ZAGATSURVEY

1995

WASHINGTON, D.C. BALTIMORE RESTAURANTS

**Edited by
Olga Boikess**

**Published and distributed by
ZAGAT**SURVEY
**4 Columbus Circle
New York, New York 10019
212 977 6000**

Acknowledgments

Besides thanking the nearly 2,700 Washington–Baltimore restaurant-goers who shared their dining experience with us, we are especially grateful to Jay Block, Tom Bryant, Al and Ellen Butts, Fred Deutsch, Gerry and Len Feinglass, Lorraine Fitzsimmons, Gail Forman, Justin, Abe, Joey and Micheline Frank, Phyllis Frucht, Jessica and Judy Greene, Jim Jacobi, Rochelle Jaffe, Barbara Johnson, Paul Kainen, Bill Kopit, Nira Long, Gordon and Ruth Shaw, George D. Stewart, Bob and Bonnie Temple, Marcia and Gary Waldorf, and the Willis family for their support. Our special thanks go to Jami Yuspa for her editorial assistance.

Contents

Introduction

Here are the results of our *1995 Washington, D.C.–Baltimore Survey* covering more than 600 restaurants in the Washington, Baltimore and Annapolis area. This year, nearly 2,700 people participated. Since the participants dined out an average of 3 times per week, this *Survey* is based on roughly 420,000 meals per year.

Knowing that the quality of this *Survey* is the direct result of their thoughtful voting and commentary, we thank each one of our participants. They include numerous professionals, business executives and just plain folks – food lovers all.

By regularly surveying large numbers of regular restaurant-goers, we think we have achieved a uniquely current and reliable guide. We hope you agree. On the assumption that most people want a "quick fix" on the places at which they are considering eating, we have tried to be concise and to provide handy indexes.

We are particularly grateful to Olga Boikess, a Washington lawyer and avid restaurant-goer, who has organized and edited this *Survey* since it was first published in the fall of 1986.

We invite you to be a reviewer in our next *Survey*. To do so, simply send a stamped, self-addressed, business-size envelope to ZAGAT SURVEY, 4 Columbus Circle, New York, NY 10019, so that we will be able to contact you. Each participant will receive a free copy of the next *Washington, D.C.–Baltimore Restaurant Survey* when it is published.

Your comments, suggestions and criticisms of this *Survey* are also solicited. There is always room for improvement with your help!

New York, New York   Nina and Tim Zagat
November 8, 1994

Foreword

We've been surveying the local dining scene since 1986 as part of our nationwide series of restaurant surveys. And every year, we're pleased to say, dining out in Washington, D.C. offers more interest and better value. Talented chefs, trained in our "ivy league" cooking schools and in the kitchens of wonderful restaurants, here and abroad, are responding to our changing lifestyles and tastes. As "eating out" (or ordering in) becomes an everyday necessity, these chefs are proving that they can feed us better, and sometimes more cheaply, than at home. As an illustration, the 420,000 meals reviewed in this *Survey* cost on average a dollar less than in our last *Survey*.

With many people spending more time in restaurant dining rooms than in their own kitchens, it's no wonder that communication between chefs and customers is improving dramatically. The overnight success of Bob Kinkead's eponymous multi-level bistro, serving pared-down versions of his modern American food, is a case in point.

Communication goes in both directions as chefs explore their culinary interests with an increasingly sophisticated dining public. Examples abound: Yannick Cam's reinvented Latin tapas at trendy Coco Loco and country French at his Provence; Nora Pouillon's wholesome ingredients and Asian techniques at Asia Nora; Gerard Pangaud's (Gerard's Place) and Jean-Louis Palladin's (Jean-Louis, Palladin) French bistros. At every dining level – from the Willard Room to corporate Clyde's – chefs are cultivating local farmers and upstream suppliers and exchanging views with their customers, downstream.

What makes restaurants "work" for everyday '90s dining is quality food in "a-meal-or-a-snack" settings. Il Radicchio, the bottomless-bowl pasta/pizzeria, and upcoming Arucola, serving family-style Italian food from rolling carts, demonstrate Roberto Donna's (Galileo, I Matti) creativity in developing such formats. Mark Caraluzzi (Bistro Bistro, D'Angelo) is equally adept.

The same stimulating changes can be seen in Baltimore where Michael Gettier (M. Gettier), Nancy Longo (Pierpoint),

Linwood Dame (Linwood's, Due) and Fernand Tersiguel (Tersiguel's) are all in command of restaurants that reflect their creativity while focusing on quality ingredients and good value. With talented chefs and restaurateurs serving an increasingly savvy market, there's even better eating ahead.

Washington, D.C.   Olga Boikess
November 8, 1994

Key to Ratings/Symbols

This sample entry identifies the various types of information contained in your Zagat Survey.

(1) Restaurant Name, Address & Phone Number

(2) Hours & Credit Cards

(3) ZAGAT Ratings

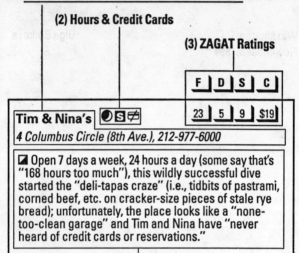

F	D	S	C
23	5	9	$19

Tim & Nina's ◐ S ⊄
4 Columbus Circle (8th Ave.), 212-977-6000

◢ Open 7 days a week, 24 hours a day (some say that's "168 hours too much"), this wildly successful dive started the "deli-tapas craze" (i.e., tidbits of pastrami, corned beef, etc. on cracker-size pieces of stale rye bread); unfortunately, the place looks like a "none-too-clean garage" and Tim and Nina have "never heard of credit cards or reservations."

(4) Surveyors' Commentary

The names of restaurants with the highest overall ratings and greatest popularity are printed in **CAPITAL LETTERS**. Address and phone numbers are printed in *italics*.

(2) Hours & Credit Cards

After each restaurant name you will find the following courtesy information:

◐ .... *serving after 11 PM*

S .... *open on Sunday*

⊄ .... *no credit cards accepted*

8

(3) ZAGAT Ratings

Food, **Decor** and **Service** are each rated on a scale of **0** to **30**:

F	D	S	C

F .... **Food**
D .... **Decor**
S .... **Service**
C .... **Cost**

13	11	14	$8

0 - 9	....	*poor to fair*
10 - 19	....	*good to very good*
20 - 25	....	*very good to excellent*
26 - 30	....	*extraordinary to perfection*

▽ 20	12	19	$16

▽ .... *Low number of votes/less reliable*

The **Cost (C)** column reflects the estimated price of a dinner with one drink and tip. Lunch usually costs 25% less.

A restaurant listed without ratings is either an important **newcomer** or a popular **write-in**. The estimated cost, with one drink and tip, is indicated by the following symbols.

			VE

I	....	*below $15*
M	....	*$16 to $30*
E	....	*$31 to $50*
VE	....	*$51 or more*

(4) Surveyors' Commentary

Surveyors' comments are summarized with literal comments shown in quotation marks. The following symbols indicate whether responses were mixed or uniform.

◪ .... *mixed comments*
◼ .... *uniform comments*

Washington's Most Popular Restaurants

Each of our reviewers has been asked to name his or her five favorite restaurants. The 40 spots most frequently named, in order of their popularity, are:

1. L'Auberge Chez Francois
2. Inn at Little Washington
3. Galileo
4. Red Sage
5. Jean-Louis
6. Citronelle
7. The Prime Rib
8. Nora
9. I Ricchi
10. Kinkead's
11. Le Lion d'Or
12. Rio Grande Cafe
13. Bombay Club
14. Morton's of Chicago
15. Obelisk
16. The Palm
17. Bice
18. Morrison-Clark Inn
19. Vidalia
20. Gerard's Place
21. Two Quail
22. Taberna del Alabardero
23. La Colline
24. Palladin
25. 1789
26. Carlyle Grand Cafe
27. Cheesecake Factory
28. 701
29. Jaleo
30. Old Angler's Inn
31. I Matti
32. Sam & Harry's
33. Duangrat's
34. Lebanese Taverna
35. City Lights of China
36. Le Gaulois
37. Old Ebbitt Grill
38. New Heights
39. Haandi
40. Austin Grill

It's obvious that most of the restaurants on the above list are among the most expensive, but Washingtonians love a bargain. Were popularity calibrated to price, we suspect that a number of other restaurants would join the above ranks. Thus, we have listed over 180 "Best Buys" on pages 16 and 17.

Top Ratings*

Top 40 Food Ranking

29 Inn/Little Washington**
27 Jean-Louis
   L'Auberge Chez Francois
26 Le Lion d'Or
   Nicholas
   Galileo
25 Prime Rib
   Kinkead's
   Seasons
   Obelisk
   Nora
   Citronelle
   Morton's of Chicago
   Morrison-Clark Inn
   Taberna del Alabardero
   Coppi's
24 Bleu Rock Inn
   Peking Gourmet Inn
   1789
   Palladin

Patisserie Cafe Didier
Trumpets
La Bergerie
I Ricchi
Gerard's Place
Coeur de Lion
Bombay Club
Jefferson
Duangrat's
Haandi
Tachibana
Melrose
Mr. K's
Pizzeria Paradiso
R.T.'s
Inn at Perry Cabin
Taste of Saigon
Le Caprice
Panjshir
Lafayette

Top Spots by Cuisine

Top American (Contemporary)
26 Nicholas
25 Kinkead's
   Seasons
   Nora
   Morrison-Clark Inn

Top Breakfast†
24 Patisserie Cafe Didier
23 La Colline
   Firehook Bakery
   Palais du Chocolat
22 La Brasserie

Top Brunch
25 Kinkead's
   Seasons
   Citronelle
   Morrison-Clark Inn
   Coppi's

Top Business Lunch
26 Le Lion d'Or
   Nicholas
   Galileo
25 Prime Rib
   Kinkead's

Top Chinese
24 Peking Gourmet Inn
   Mr. K's
23 City Lights of China
22 China Canteen
   Fortune

Top Continental
24 Restaurant, RC, Tysons
23 Grill, RC, Pent.
   Jockey Club
22 Tivoli
   Powerscourt

---

* Excluding restaurants with low voting.
**Over an hour away.
† Other than hotels.

Top Creole/Cajun/New Orleans
24 R.T.'s
21 Warehouse Grill
20 Cajun Bangkok
Louisiana Express

Top Family Dining
22 Rio Grande Cafe
21 Red Hot & Blue
Tomato Palace
20 D'Angelo
19 Union St. Public Hse.

Top French Bistro
24 Palladin
Le Caprice
Le Refuge
La Cote d'Or Cafe
23 La Colline

Top French Classic
27 L'Auberge Chez Francois
26 Le Lion d'Or
24 Palladin
La Bergerie
Le Caprice

Top French (New)
27 Jean-Louis
25 Citronelle
24 Gerard's Place
23 Maison Blanche
22 Le Mistral

Top Hamburgers
22 Occidental Grill
Carlyle Grand Cafe
20 Artie's
Houston's
19 Old Ebbitt Grill

Top of the Hill
23 La Colline
22 La Brasserie
Le Mistral
Powerscourt
Two Quail

Top Hotel Dining
27 Jean-Louis/Watergate
26 Nicholas/Mayflower
25 Seasons/Four Seasons
Citronelle/Latham
Morrison-Clark Inn

Top Indian
24 Bombay Club
Haandi
23 Bombay Bistro
22 Bombay Palace
Aditi

Top Italian
26 Galileo
25 Obelisk
24 I Ricchi
Vincenzo
23 Il Pizzico

Top Japanese
24 Tachibana
Hisago
23 Sushi-Ko
Tako Grill
22 Matuba

Top Mexican
22 Rio Grande Cafe
21 Enriqueta's
20 Tortilla Factory
19 Tia Queta
Austin Grill

Top Middle Eastern
22 Nizam's
Bacchus
Kazan
21 Eye St. Cafe
17 Iron Gate

Top Newcomers/Rated
25 Kinkead's
Coppi's
24 Palladin
Gerard's Place
23 Pesce

12

Top Newcomers/Unrated
Asia Nora
Coco Loco
Oval Room
Provence
Rupperts

Top Pizza
25 Coppi's
24 Pizzeria Paradiso
21 Eye St. Cafe
Tomato Palace
Il Radicchio

Top Seafood
23 Pesce
22 Blue Point Grill
21 Sea Catch
Crisfield
Falls Landing

Top Southeast Asian
23 Straits of Malaya
22 Germaine's
19 Pan Asian Noodles
— Asia Nora

Top Southern
25 Morrison-Clark Inn
24 Jefferson
Vidalia
21 Georgia Brown's
14 Dixie Grill

Top Southwestern
22 Red Sage
Santa Fe East
Rio Grande Cafe
20 Cottonwood Cafe
19 Austin Grill

Top Steakhouses
25 Prime Rib
Morton's of Chicago
23 Sam & Harry's
Palm, The
22 Ruth's Chris

Top Tapas
25 Taberna del Alabardero
23 Jaleo
22 Terramar
19 Gabriel
— Coco Loco

Top Thai
24 Duangrat's
22 Busara
Crystal Thai
Bua
21 Thai Flavor

Top Vietnamese
24 Taste of Saigon
22 Queen Bee
Saigon Gourmet
East Wind
Cafe Dalat

Top Worth a Trip
29 Inn/Little Washington/
Washington, VA
24 Bleu Rock Inn/Paris, VA
Inn at Perry Cabin/
St. Michaels, MD
— Imperial Hotel,
Chestertown, MD
— Willow Grove Inn,
Orange, VA

Top 40 Decor Ranking

28	Inn/Little Washington	Melrose
27	Willard Room	Jockey Club
26	L'Auberge Chez Francois	Jefferson
	Inn at Perry Cabin	Sequoia
	Coeur de Lion	701
	Red Sage	Mr. K's
	Taberna del Alabardero	Prime Rib
25	Lafayette	Le Lion d'Or
	Colonnade, The	Busara
	1789	*23* Two Quail
	Seasons	Nora
	Nicholas	Galileo
	Grill, RC, Pent.	La Bergerie
	Bombay Club	Occidental Grill
	Morrison-Clark Inn	Coppi's
	Restaurant, RC, Tysons	New Heights
	Old Angler's Inn	Hibiscus Cafe
24	Bleu Rock Inn	Palladin
	Jean-Louis	Hisago
	Allegro	River Club

Top Outdoor

Bleu Rock Inn	Perry's
Coco Loco	Sequoia
Fleetwood's	701
La Brasserie	Straits of Malaya
L'Auberge Chez Francois	Tom Tom
Old Angler's Inn	Willow Grove Inn

Top Rooms

Asia Nora	Nicholas
Bombay Club	Provence
Coeur de Lion	Red Sage
Grill, RC, Pent.	Restaurant, RC, Tysons
Inn/Little Washington	Seasons
Jean-Louis	1789
Jockey Club	Taberna del Alabardero
Morrison-Clark Inn	Willard Room

Top Views

Chart House	Le Rivage
Fleetwood's	Perry's
Gangplank	Potowmack Landing
L'Auberge Chez Francois	Sequoia

Top 40 Service Ranking

28 Inn/Little Washington
26 L'Auberge Chez Francois
Jean-Louis
25 Nicholas
Le Lion d'Or
Coeur de Lion
Seasons
Bleu Rock Inn
Taberna del Alabardero
24 Prime Rib
1789
Jefferson
Willard Room
Inn at Perry Cabin
23 Nora
Melrose
Morrison-Clark Inn
Bombay Club
La Bergerie
Obelisk

Lafayette
Jockey Club
Grill, RC, Pent.
Mr. K's
701
Galileo
Colonnade, The
Palladin
Morton's of Chicago
Restaurant, RC, Tysons
22 Kinkead's
Gerard's Place
Trumpets
Sam & Harry's
La Cote d'Or Cafe
Citronelle
Taste of Saigon
Tivoli
Maison Blanche
Le Refuge

Best Buys*

Top 100 Bangs For The Buck

This list reflects the best dining values in our *Survey*. It is produced by dividing the cost of a meal into the combined ratings for food, decor and service.

1. Bob & Edith's Diner
2. Coppi's
3. C.F. Folks
4. Pho 75
5. Hard Times Cafe
6. Crisp & Juicy
7. Generous George's
8. Patisserie Cafe Didier
9. China Canteen
10. Taste of Saigon
11. Delhi Dhaba
12. Calvert Grille
13. Il Forno
14. Crystal Thai
15. Faccia Luna
16. Food Factory
17. Dean & DeLuca Cafe
18. Tortilla Factory
19. Cafe Dalat
20. Bertucci's
21. China Chef
22. Silver Diner
23. Florida Ave. Grill
24. Il Pizzico
25. Bombay Bistro
26. Pizzeria Paradiso
27. Polly's Cafe
28. Pan Asian Noodles
29. Bua
30. Nam Viet
31. Eye St. Cafe
32. Anita's
33. Austin Grill
34. Queen Bee
35. Houston's
36. Red Hot & Blue
37. Hunan Number One
38. Panjshir
39. Meskerem
40. Aditi
41. Ledo Pizza
42. Thai Place
43. Good Fortune
44. El Tamarindo
45. City Lights of China
46. Haandi
47. Seven Seas
48. Hamburger Hamlet
49. Rio Grande Cafe
50. Full Kee
51. Busara
52. Hard Rock Cafe
53. Thai Taste
54. Hunan Chinatown
55. Il Radicchio
56. Mick's
57. Mike's Amer. Grill
58. Sabang
59. Sala Thai
60. Artie's
61. Duangrat's
62. Fortune
63. Old Glory BBQ
64. Bangkok Orchid
65. Jade Palace
66. Geppetto
67. Ecco Cafe
68. Union St. Public Hse.
69. Skewers
70. Ivy's Place
71. Saigon Gourmet
72. Mixtec
73. Bistro Le Monde
74. Thai Kingdom
75. Cactus Cantina
76. Dixie Grill
77. Carlyle Grand Cafe
78. Cajun Bangkok
79. Montego Cafe
80. Straits of Malaya
81. Foong Lin
82. Louisiana Express
83. Bilbo Baggins
84. Four Rivers
85. T.G.I. Friday's
86. Lebanese Taverna
87. Planet Hollywood
88. Tortilla Coast
89. Cheesecake Factory
90. Atlacatl
91. Capitol City Brewing Co.
92. Pines of Italy
93. Chadwicks
94. Matuba
95. Bangkok Gourmet
96. East Wind
97. Hinode
98. Jaleo
99. Outback Steakhse.
100. Enriqueta's

---

* Excluding coffeehouses.

16

Additional Good Values
(A bit more expensive, but worth every penny)

Aangan	Lite 'n' Fair
American Cafe	Little Fountain Cafe
Andalucia	Martin's Tavern
Appetizer Plus	Miss Saigon
Asia Nora	Montgomery's Grille
Bamiyan	Mr. Yung's
Bistro Bistro	Music City Roadhouse
Bistro Bravo	Nam's
Bistro Français	Notte Luna
Bombay Club	Odeon Cafe
Boss Cats	Old Ebbitt Grill
Burma	Palais du Chocolat
Cafe Atlantico	Paolo's
Cafe Petitto	Pasha Cafe
Cambodian	Pasta Plus
Chicken Place	Peking Gourmet Inn
Cities	Perry's
Clyde's	Pesce
Connaught Place	Pilin Thai
D'Angelo	Pines of Rome
Dfouny	Pleasant Peasant
Eat First	R.T.'s
Fern St. Bistro	Rupperts
Firehook Bakery	Sakura Palace
Garden Cafe	Santa Fe East
Gulf Coast Kitchen	Starke's BBQ
Havana Cafe	State of the Union
Head's	Stella's
Hibiscus Cafe	Sunny Garden
Hsiang Foong	Tabard Inn
Ichiban	Tachibana
I Matti	Taipei/Tokyo Cafe
Kazan	Tako Grill
Kramerbooks/Afterwords	Tavola
la Madeleine	Thai Flavor
Lauriol Plaza	That's Amore
Lavandou	Tia Queta
Le Bon Cafe	Tom Tom
Le Gaulois	Tomato Palace
Listrani's	Wurzburg-Haus

Alphabetical
Directory
of Restaurants

Aangan [S] – | – | – | M

4920 St. Elmo Ave. (bet. Old Georgetown Rd. & Norfolk Ave.), Bethesda, MD, 301-657-1262

A soothing courtyard ambiance enhanced by "VIP" hospitality makes diners feel like they're in colonial India far removed from busy Bethesda; and yet this newcomer's vegetarian and tandoori dishes are attuned to modern health-conscious tastes.

Aditi [S] 22 | 17 | 19 | $18

3299 M St., NW (33rd St.), 202-625-6825

◪ Good-value "feasts" at this Georgetown Indian feature some "excellent" tandoori and vegetarian choices, dressed-up digs and "quirky" (i.e., "when/if") service; most consider it "an all-round good experience" but not up to its rave reviews.

Alekos [S] 18 | 12 | 17 | $20

1732 Connecticut Ave., NW (bet. S & R Sts.), 202-667-6211

■ DC may lack distinguished Greek food, but generous Hellenic hospitality pervades this homey storefront above Dupont Circle; here locals rub elbows with "conventioneers from Dubuque" as everyone digs into "huge portions" of "delicious" lamb or swordfish; "order less", you get more.

Allegro [S] 21 | 24 | 22 | $30

Sheraton Carlton Hotel, 923 16th St., NW (K St.), 202-879-6900

■ A "magnificent" neo-classical hotel dining room with "fine", if pricey, Contemporary American dining, "service with a European touch" and lighting that "makes 40ish look 30ish"; only two blocks from the White House yet often overlooked, it's a "favorite last-minute spot" for savvy lunchers and a stately backdrop for a deal.

America ◐ [S] 15 | 18 | 16 | $19

Union Station, 50 Mass. Ave., NE (North Capitol), 202-682-9555
Tysons Corner Ctr., 8008 L Tysons Corner Ctr. (Rte. 7), McLean, VA, 703-847-6607

◪ Showcasing "Capitol views" and a pedestrian "parade", this sprawling "upscale" Union Station diner with its "diverse-as-America" menu attracts everyone from Senators to tourists with tired tots; an operation this big is bound to be "impersonal" and "uneven", but both food and service are "surprisingly ok"; the new Tysons Corner behemoth (not rated) has similar plates, fewer pols.

American Cafe [S]

F	D	S	C
15	14	15	$16

227 Mass. Ave., NE (2nd St.), 202-547-8500
1211 Wisconsin Ave., NW (bet. M & N Sts.), 202-944-9464
The Shops at National Pl., 1331 Pennsylvania Ave., NW (bet. 13th & F Sts.), 202-626-0770
Ballston Commons Mall, 4238 Wilson Blvd. (Glebe Rd.), Arlington, VA, 703-522-2236
5252 Wisconsin Ave., NW (Jennifer St.), 202-363-5400 🌙
8601 Westwood Ctr. (Rte. 7), Vienna, VA, 703-848-9476
11835 Fair Oaks Mall, Fairfax, VA, 703-352-0368
1200 19th St., NW (bet. M & N Sts.), 202-223-2121

◩ Why did 900 surveyors choose one of these "mediocre places"?; "AmCafs" have "something for everyone" and are "easy places for decent food" where you "know what to expect"; in addition, they offer a "bright atmosphere", "late-night dining" and are "cheap"; let's go.

Andalucia [S]

F	D	S	C
21	17	21	$27

12300 Wilkens Ave. (Parklawn Dr.), Rockville, MD, 301-770-1880
The Shoppes of Bethesda, 9431 Elm St. (Arlington Rd.), Bethesda, MD, 301-907-0052

■ "Authentic" feeling Spanish tavernas, in Rockville and Bethesda, serving "simple but good" classics like zarzuella and paella with a blend of formality and friendliness, accompanied by a "magnificent guitarist"; it makes "a nice evening out" – "in the suburbs, yet."

Anita's [S]

F	D	S	C
15	9	15	$12

147 W. Maple Ave. (bet. Lawyer's & Old Court Rds.), Vienna, VA, 703-938-0888
521 E. Maple Ave. (East St.), Vienna, VA, 703-255-1001 🌙
10880 Lee Hwy. (Rtes. 50 & 123), Fairfax, VA, 703-385-2965
9278 Old Keene Mill Rd. (Shiplett Rd.), Burke, VA, 703-455-3466
701 Elden St. (Dranesville), Herndon, VA, 703-481-1441 🌙
13921 Lee Jackson Hwy. (Centreville Rd.), Chantilly, VA, 703-378-1717
10611 Lomond Dr. (Rte. 234), Manassas, VA, 703-335-6400

◩ Northern Virginians gripe that they "ditched the homemade flavor" and the "homey charm" of the East Vienna "original" when this New Mexican became a chain of "Tex-Mex truck stops"; still, they're "cheap, filling", "better than most" of their type and open for breakfast.

Appetizer Plus [S]

F	D	S	C
16	8	15	$18

1117 N. 19th St. (Lynn St.), Rosslyn, VA, 703-525-3171

◩ This "accommodating" Rosslyn all-you-can-eat buffet sushi bar is a "good deal" if you'll settle for "competent" if uninspired sushi on an "Asian smorgasbord"; come hungry, "bring your teenagers" and plan to wait since this bargain is no secret.

Armadilla Grill   15 16 16 $19
1421 Sulleyfield Circle (Rte. 50), Chantilly, VA, 703-631-9332
8011 Woodmont Ave. (Cordell Ave.), Bethesda, MD,
301-907-9637 🅂
◪ An amiable separation of these "interesting" New
Mexican grills (rated together above) lets founder Joyce
Piotrowski focus on the "charming", off-beat Virginia
location where her "authentic" SW and Native American
specials attract acclaim; there's been no major change in
the Bethesda location – it's still handy "when Rio
Grande's full."

Artie's ◐🅂   20 17 19 $19
3260 Old Lee Hwy. (south of Fairfax Circle), Fairfax, VA,
703-273-7600
◪ "Waits" and "noise" – the main complaints about this
"chummy" Fairfax American bar and grill – indicate its
success in filling a suburban Virginia void with a "wide-
ranging" menu of sandwiches, salads and light entrees,
backed by an upscale setting, smiling faces and "late" hours.

Asia Nora   – – – M
2213 M St., NW (bet. 22nd & 23rd Sts.), 202-797-4860
Healthy eating takes an exciting Asian twist at Nora
Pouillon's new West End venture highlighting wholesome
ingredients and creativity in Far Eastern flavors and
techniques; look for dishes like rotisserie Szechuan duck,
noodle tasting platters and meal-sized soups in a
seductive, house-in-the-Asian-countryside setting.

Atami 🅂   20 11 18 $21
3155 Wilson Blvd. (Clarendon Metro Stop), Arlington, VA,
703-522-4787
■ Although this small, "straightforward" Japanese-
Vietnamese is known for its $24.95 all-you-can-eat sushi
deal, Arlington regulars tout its "great" sukiyaki or sushi
"off the menu"; it's not fancy enough for an important
evening, but it caters special events.

Atlacatl 🅂   17 8 14 $14
2602 Columbia Pike (Walter Reed Dr.), Arlington, VA,
703-920-3680
■ Though it's "still worth going" to this cheap, crowded
Arlington dive for its fried yuca chips, puposas and other
"distinctive" Salvadoran appetizers, reports of "erratic"
food and service that matches the "rough" setting explain
why it's "lost appeal."

22

Austin Grill 🅂   19 | 16 | 17 | $16 |
2404 Wisconsin Ave., NW (Calvert St.), 202-337-8080
South Austin Grill 🅂
801 King St. (Washington St.), Alexandria, VA, 703-684-8969
■ It's not just the "festive" ambiance that "makes it worth
the wait" at these jam-packed "Texas roadhouses" in
Upper Georgetown and Old Town; the salsas and SW
dishes are fresh-tasting and "user-friendly" ("not
overwhelmed with fat or cheese"), and, while the
"margaritas are on the sour side, the help isn't."

Bacchus   22 | 18 | 20 | $23 |
1827 Jefferson Place, NW (bet. M & N Sts.), 202-785-0734
7945 Norfolk Ave. (Del Ray Ave.), Bethesda, MD,
301-657-1722 🅂
■ Sampling a tableful of meze (Middle Eastern tapas) at
these attractive Lebanese siblings transforms an ordinary
meal into a "banquet"; you may "never make it past the
appetizers", but the "helpful" staff will suggest tasty entrees.

Bamiyan 🅂   21 | 15 | 18 | $20 |
3320 M St., NW (bet. 33rd & 34th Sts.), 202-338-1896
300 King St. (Fairfax St.), Alexandria, VA, 703-548-9006
🅉 Many meat-and-potato types "never knew they liked
Afghan food" before trying these ethnic pioneers;
although still worthwhile, we hear that their "age is
starting to show" in slightly "seedy" locations (now under
separate management).

Bangkok Gourmet 🅂   21 | 14 | 19 | $20 |
523 S. 23rd St. (Rte. 1), Arlington, VA, 703-521-1305
🅉 Thai chef "Pat" Phatiphond's "innovative" French-Thai
food "warrants numerous visits" to this "charming little
place" in Arlington; however, appreciation of his
"originality" is tempered by a feeling that he's been
"eclipsed" by showier Thai newcomers.

Bangkok Orchid 🅂   18 | 15 | 17 | $17 |
301 Mass. Ave., NE (3rd St.), 202-546-5900
🅉 Finding "affordable prices", "appealing surroundings",
"outdoor seating" and a Thai kitchen "with flair" on
Capitol Hill is "delightful"; however, this Thai may also be
"inconsistent"; busy at lunch, it's empty at night.

Baron's   ▽ 19 | 23 | 22 | $33 |
Sheraton Premiere at Tysons Corner, 8661 Leesburg Pike
(Rte. 267), Vienna, VA, 703-448-1234
🅉 A "gorgeous old-world setting" is the backdrop for
"creatively presented" Contemporary Continental food at
this Tysons Corner dining room; not too many of our
surveyors know it, but those who do are impressed: "good
for a hotel in the suburbs."

BeDuCi 22 | 21 | 22 | $28

2014 P St., NW (bet. 20th & 21st Sts.), 202-467-4466

◪ Aspiring, some say "overambitious", cozy Mediterranean located *Be*low *Du*pont *Ci*rcle; praise for its "inventive" "unforced cooking", "delicious" pasta and "friendly" staff is matched by comments like: "too many ingredients", "too chatty", "no excuse for going."

Belmont Kitchen [S] 20 | 18 | 18 | $22

2400 18th St., NW (Belmont Rd.), 202-667-1200

■ This "enduring" Adams Morgan "gathering place" is popular for "leisurely" brunches on the streetside patio and intimate dining in dark nooks indoors; its American "yuppie food" (defined by upside-down pizzas) tastes "good even when you're served something you didn't order."

Bertucci's [S] 18 | 16 | 16 | $15

2000 Pennsylvania Ave., NW (bet. 20th & 21st Sts.), 202-296-2600

13195 Parcher Ave. (bet. Elden St. & Worldgate Dr.), Herndon, VA, 703-787-6500

◪ This multi-location, Boston pizza maker turns "brick-oven", "custom pizza" into '90s "fast food"; it's a welcome family option where "parents can have seafood and pasta and the kids, pizza", and also appeals to students and shoppers "tired of ordinary" pies; however, it's "Russian roulette on service."

BICE [S] 22 | 22 | 20 | $36

601 Pennsylvania Ave., NW (Indiana Ave.), 202-638-2423

■ "A lot of Clintonites" have found this "boisterous" Downtown Milanese "convenient to the Hill for votes"; its "delicious" pastas and risottos are especially "good on someone else's tab" and, despite gripes about snobby help, "when the kitchen connects, it's a gem."

Bilbo Baggins [S] 20 | 19 | 19 | $20

208 Queen St. (Lee St.), Alexandria, VA, 703-683-0300

■ A "warm, woody, Berkeley"-in-the-'60s feeling pervades this "Old Town charmer"; its legendary homemade raisin bread and sticky buns are as much a lure as its reliable American and veggie dishes and new wine bar.

Bistro Bistro [S] 20 | 19 | 19 | $21

Village at Shirlington, 4021 S. 28th St., Arlington, VA, 703-379-0300

◪ One of several busy "American-style bistros" in upscale Shirlington with a wide-ranging menu but "inconsistent" service; what makes more than one reviewer "glad I finally tried it" is the "quality of ingredients", its salads and desserts; dissenters "yawn."

Bistro Bravo [S] ▽ 18 | 15 | 14 | $15
1301 Connecticut Ave., NW (N St. & Dupont Circle), 202-223-3300
◪ This sunny French crêperie near Dupont Circle turns out "magnificent" crêpes; however, since its expansion service lags, and the new bistro specials prompt the question how "could such a swell-sounding menu be so poorly cooked?"; "bistro yes, bravo no."

Bistro Français ◐ [S] 20 | 17 | 18 | $25
3128 M St., NW (bet. 31st St. & Wisconsin Ave.), 202-338-3830
◪ Bustling French brasserie in Georgetown (though it feels "like Paris"), whose standout roast chicken, pommes frites, steak tartare, late hours (open till 3 AM – 4 AM weekends) and Gallic "attitude" are a "staple" of DC dining; check out the daily prix fixe menus for "good deals."

Bistro Le Monde [S] 18 | 16 | 17 | $17
223 Pennsylvania Ave., SE (bet. 2nd & 3rd Sts.), 202-544-4153
■ This crowded "faux French" bistro proves that "a few dishes well done", and a handy location "for Congressional staff", is all that's needed to succeed on the Hill – especially with "good house wine" offsetting "slow French service."

Bistro Twenty Fifteen [S] (fka Lucie) – | – | – | M
Embassy Row Hotel, 2015 Mass. Ave. (off Dupont Circle), 202-939-4250
An "elegant" hotel dining room off Dupont Circle that was recently reformatted into a less pricey, modern American bistro with a relaxed (if a bit "impersonal") setting and a menu accommodating everything from a snack to a celebration; hopefully, service has also loosened up.

BLEU ROCK INN [S] 24 | 24 | 25 | $39
U.S. Route 211 (5 mi. west of Hwy. 522 North), Washington, VA, 703-987-3190
◪ In a "romantic setting" with a "million dollar view" of the Blue Ridge Mountains, this "comfortable" country inn offers a "getaway at a good price"; but since the French-accented American food and service don't compare to the nearby Inn at Little Washington (or even Four and Twenty Blackbirds), the question is: for the same drive, "why go third best?"

Blue Point Grill 22 | 17 | 20 | $28
600 Franklin St. (S. Washington St.), Alexandria, VA, 703-739-0404
◪ An abundance of fresh seafood makes a "brunch worth catching" at this finfare-focused cafe adjacent to Sutton Place Gourmet in Alexandria; at dinner, plain surroundings and "inconsistencies" show that it still has kinks.

Bob & Edith's Diner ◐ [S] 💳̸ 15 | 11 | 17 | $9

2310 Columbia Pike (Wayne St.), Arlington, VA, 703-920-6103

◪ This "typical greasy spoon", with the accent on "greasy", gets raves for its diner fare being "cheap"; though open at 3 AM and more entertaining than the *Late Show*, for many, its "authenticity wears thin with food this mediocre."

Bombay Bistro [S] 23 | 12 | 19 | $16

Bell's Corner, 98 W. Montgomery Ave. (Washington St.), Rockville, MD, 301-762-8798

■ The daily lineup (even "in the cold") outside this modest Rockville Indian is the best endorsement of its talented kitchen not to mention the drawing power of its "cordial service"; the $5.95 weekday lunch buffet, with lots of "interesting selections", is a steal.

BOMBAY CLUB [S] 24 | 25 | 23 | $31

815 Connecticut Ave. (bet. H & I Sts.), 202-659-3727

■ Rated the "best Indian in town", the "royal treatment", "restrained atmosphere" and "subtle" dishes at this "classy" relic of the British Raj is a "client-dinner dream"; though only a block from the White House (and, reputedly, a Chelsea Clinton choice), it has bipartisan support: "great even though the Democrats seem to think so too."

Bombay Palace [S] 22 | 21 | 20 | $25

2020 K St., NW (bet. 20th & 21st Sts.), 202-331-4200

◪ Despite its move across K Street to fancier digs, this link in an international Indian chain still "lacks the panache of Bombay Club" (with which it's sometimes confused); however, it's favored by many locals and their "Indian friends" for its fire and spice, and vegetarian choices.

Boss Cats [S] – | – | – | I

5872 Leesburg Pike (west of Columbia Pike), Bailey's Crossroads, VA, 703-845-9800

Billed as an "urban beach bar" with a colorful seashore motif, this Falls Church newcomer is a snack-o-rama of updated, nutritionally savvy bar nibbles and diner specials, scripted high spirits and built-in kid appeal that's found its niche as a "nice family place."

Bua [S] 22 | 18 | 19 | $18

1635 P St. (bet. 16th & 17th Sts.), 202-265-0828

■ Altogether "a delightful dining experience" sums up this "in-town" Thai whose "discreet decor" and "courteous" manners contrast with its "incendiary" dishes; when the few "wonderful tables overlooking P Street" are occupied or when there's a "wait on a weeknight", consider the "consistently good" takeout.

Buon Giorno　　　–　–　–　M

8003 Norfolk Ave. (Del Ray Ave.), Bethseda, MD, 301-652-1400
"A solid Italian where nobody speaks Italian" including
most of its Bethseda customers; the "large tables" in its
"gracious", flower-filled dining rooms are perfect for
friendly get-togethers, and the seafood, veal chop and
pasta aren't bad either.

Burma Restaurant ⓢ　　　–　–　–　I

740 Sixth St., NW (bet. H & G Sts.), 202-638-1280
If the closest you've been to Burma is a "Road to
Mandalay" rerun, follow our adventurous surveyors to
this "entrancing" spot "hidden upstairs" in Chinatown; its
"distinctive" green tea salad and squid are only some of
the "beautifully seasoned choices"; expect to stay awhile.

Busara ⓢ　　　22　24　21　$22

2340 Wisconsin Ave., NW (Calvert St.), 202-337-2340
■ "High-tech, funk" decor is paired with "Cal-Thai" food
at this "avant-garde" Asian in Upper Georgetown; though
some prefer the food at its "homelier" siblings (Bua and
Tara Thai), nothing beats the "refreshing" courtyard "for
summer dining"; live jazz and walking scenery make it a
"late-night hot spot."

Cactus Cantina ⓢ　　　18　16　16　$17

3300 Wisconsin Ave., NW (Macomb St.), 202-686-7222
☑ "Always packed", this "festive" Cleveland Park
cantina's "sturdy margaritas", "homemade tortillas" and
"awesome fajitas" get lower ratings but draw nearly as
big a crowd as "its prototype, Rio Grande Cafe"; go
"off-hours for the food" (it's not as "brusque") and, in
summer, for some of the "best sidewalk seats" in town.

Cafe Atlantico ⓢ　　　20　21　18　$23

*1819 Columbia Rd. (bet. Biltmore & Mintwood Sts.),
202-328-5844*
■ A "bit of (Miami's) South Beach", with an open-to-the-
street party "atmosphere and music unrivaled" elsewhere in
Adams Morgan; its "cosmopolitan" clientele come for tasty
Caribbean tapas or dinner, then dance the night away.

Cafe BaBaLu ⓢ　　　–　–　–　M

*3235 M St., NW (across from Georgetown Park),
202-965-5353*
A second-tier tapas tyro with a trendy menu; its air of
informality catches tourists and youngsters looking for the
raucous M Street dance club that used to occupy these
premises, but notwithstanding its pre-opening ballyhoo,
bringing rooftop dining to Georgetown is its main innovation.

Cafe Berlin S   20 | 16 | 18 | $22
322 Mass. Ave., NE (bet. 3rd & 4th Sts.), 202-543-7656
☑ "Pleasant" outdoor dining enhances "marvelous potato pancakes", schnitzel, spaetzle and mit schlag desserts at this "neighborhood feeling" German on Capitol Hill; seating indoors is knee-to-knee "romantic"; service happens in "fits and starts."

Cafe Bethesda   22 | 19 | 20 | $31
5027 Wilson Ln. (bet. Old Georgetown & Arlington Rds.), Bethesda, MD, 301-657-3383
☑ Fin fans find a "lot of potential" at this "intimate" French spot (in an "unexpected" Bethesda location) citing its "skillful" seafood preparations; critics carp about "teeny tiny" everything, especially the "limited" menu.

Cafe Dalat S   22 | 8 | 19 | $14
3143 Wilson Blvd. (Highland Blvd.), Arlington, VA, 703-276-0935
■ Customers are "treated as family" at this "down-home Vietnamese" in Little Saigon; its premises may "look like an old shoe store", but its kitchen could make a shoe box taste "delicious" – and the prices are so low, they're practically giving the "fresh food" away.

Cafe Milano ◑ S   19 | 18 | 15 | $29
3251 Prospect St., NW (bet. Wisconsin Ave. & 33rd St.), 202-333-6183
☑ With 15 minutes of fame produced by Marlene Chalmer Cook's after-dinner escapades, this mobbed Georgetown watering hole may just be "too hip for its own good"; the fact that lunchers (and early diners) report "imaginative, light, well-prepared" pastas, pizzas and salads is encouraging; it also has lovely outdoor space.

Cafe Mozart S   16 | 12 | 16 | $17
1331 H St., NW (bet. 13th & 14th Sts.), 202-347-5732
☑ Maybe it's "not a health haven", but this Downtown deli/restaurant is one of the few local places for hearty German food; if the "noisy", overbright ambiance in the back-room restaurant isn't your idea of gemütlichkeit, up front is a treasure trove of hard-to-find ingredients so you can do-it-yourself at home.

Cafe Petitto ◑ S   17 | 14 | 16 | $20
1724 Connecticut Ave., NW (bet. R & S Sts.), 202-462-8771
☑ Followers of fried pizza (it's not for everyone) jam this Dupont Circle "dive", stack antipasti on the one permitted plate and claim the tight seating can be "romantic"; critics say "easier on the oil" and "be more attentive"; there's a dessert bar downstairs.

Cafe Pierre S   – | – | – | E
Loews L'Enfant Plaza Hotel, 480 L'Enfant Plaza, SW,
202-484-1000
At a busy DC crossroads, near government agencies,
museums and offices, is one of the best New American
restaurants that "no one can find"; well-suited to business
and social meetings, this subdued hotel dining room is
worth seeking out for its daily menus based on fresh,
regional ingredients.

Cafe Saigon S   20 | 12 | 17 | $16
1135 N. Highland St. (bet. Wilson & Clarendon Blvds.),
Arlington, VA, 703-276-7110
☑ Holding its own against "tough competition in 'Little
Saigon'", this "funny little" "second-tier" Vietnamese
storefront delivers good, cheap soups and seafood from
a "varied" menu; "dodging smokers is difficult."

Cajun Bangkok S   20 | 11 | 19 | $17
907 King St. (Alford St.), Alexandria, VA, 703-836-0038
■ An "odd couple" – Cajun-Thai – but the juxtaposition
"works" in this "nice" Old Town storefront, largely
because its Thai owner, trained in local Cajun kitchens,
cooks each "delicious" dish authentically, and there's
"very attentive, pleasant service."

California Pizza Kitchen S   – | – | – | I
Tysons Corner Ctr., 7939-L Tysons Corner (Rte. 7), McLean,
VA, 703-761-1473
Montgomery Mall, 7101 Democracy Blvd. (Westlake Dr.),
Bethesda, MD 301-469-5090
Chevy Chase Pavilion, 5345 Wisconsin Ave., NW (Military
Rd.), 202-363-6650
These stylish, modern mall-based pizzerias give a "very
California" spin to pizzas with unusual toppings, as well as
"yummy salads", pastas and simple grills; their appeal –
"guiltless eating of food you love" – is near universal.

Calvert Grille S   19 | 12 | 20 | $14
The Calvert Apts., 3106 Mt. Vernon Ave. (bet. E & W Glebe
& Commonwealth Ave.), Alexandria, VA, 703-836-8425
■ Genuine "small-town atmosphere" fills this neighborhood
"family place" in Alexandria; the "people are friendly" and
the food "cheap"; with so many places simulating homestyle
"blue-plate" dining, it's refreshing to find the real thing.

Cambodian   ▽ 20 | 14 | 20 | $15
1727 Wilson Blvd. (Quinn St.), Arlington, VA, 703-522-3832
☑ The subtle, fiery dishes of Cambodia are more
"interesting" than the "mainstream Chinese" at this
"pleasant" ethnic in an Arlington strip mall; stuffed pork
and flounder are recommended, but the "fondue is a must."

Cantina Romana S   ▽ 22 | 21 | 23 | $35
3251 Prospect St., NW (bet. Wisconsin Ave. & 33rd St.),
202-337-5130
◧ With a "gardenlike" patio that's an "oasis of calm in
Georgetown" and a "relaxing" ambiance enhanced by
"attentive staff", admirers don't understand why this
Northern Italian gets "overlooked"; possibly because
some find the food "heavy" and "too pricey."

Capitol City Brewing Company S   14 | 19 | 15 | $17
1100 New York Ave., NW (bet. H & 11th Sts.), 202-628-2222
◧ "Brew", "babes" and "burgers" are the nighttime
attractions at this "loud and crowded" microbrewery
where the pretzels and mustard are the "best part of the
meal"; lawyer jokes can get you sued at lunch.

Carlyle Grand Cafe S   22 | 21 | 20 | $22
4000 S. 28th St. (Quincy St.), Shirlington, VA, 703-931-0777
▪ "Count on" finding "all-around good" American food at
a "fair price" at this wildly popular Shirlington bistro;
possibly because it's "not a five-star restaurant" and doesn't
try to be one, this place "always exceeds expectations."

Carnegie Deli S   15 | 9 | 12 | $14
Embassy Suites Hotel, 8517 Leesburg Pike, Tysons Corner,
VA, 703-790-5001
◧ Though it tastes pretty much like the real thing, this
Tysons Corner transplant "pales in comparison" to
nostalgic NYers' memories; despite "monumental" corned
beef and pastrami sandwiches, the waiters, who "don't
know from deli", are too nice and the "antiseptic" hotel
lobby too civilized.

Celadon S   ▽ 21 | 24 | 20 | $33
JW Marriott Hotel, 1331 Pennsylvania Ave., NW (bet. 13th
& 14th Sts.), 202-393-0361
▪ This "elegant place" for prix fixe, pre-theater dining
near the National Theatre is one of DC's few secrets; it
looks "lovely" and the French-accented food is "fine" –
service is the weak point, as in "seating is quick, but then
comes isolation."

C.F. Folks ⊄   21 | 8 | 18 | $11
1225 19th St., NW (bet. M & N Sts.), 202-293-0162
▪ It's a toss-up whether the Eclectic specials "served with
easy attitude" at this Dupont Circle lunch counter/sidewalk
cafe are "as interesting as the clientele"; the former
range from burritos to bouillabaisse, the latter, bikers to
World Bankers; closed after 3 PM and on weekends.

Chadwicks ◐ 🅢 | 14 | 14 | 16 | $16 |
5247 Wisconsin Ave., NW (Jennifer St.), 202-362-8040
3205 K St., NW (Wisconsin Ave.), 202-333-2565
203 Strand St. (Prince St.), Alexandria, VA, 703-836-4442
Hampton Inn, 9421 Largo Dr. W. (Graden Way), Landover,
MD, 301-808-0200
■ The persistent appeal of these '70s-era fern bars is that
they are "everyday, comfortable" places for "dinner
before a movie", "drinks with the gang" or a "$5 lunch";
the bar food and service seldom rise above "average",
but the "free balloons for kids" may.

Chardonnay 🅢 ▽ 20 | 20 | 17 | $29 |
Doubletree Park Terrace Hotel, 1515 Rhode Island Ave.,
NW (Scott Circle), 202-232-7000
☑ A classic courtyard and "classy" dining room provide
"delightful ambiance" for a "quiet business lunch" just off
Scott Circle; if you're into "inventive American cuisine",
getting "major portions" at moderate prices may make
you a regular.

Chart House 🅢 | 20 | 21 | 19 | $26 |
1 Cameron St. (on the water), Alexandria, VA, 703-684-5080
☑ Quintessential "rooms with a view" – besides "great
locations", this "formulaic" seafood and steakhouse
chain also has "enthusiastic" help, "spacious seating",
and "brunch lines that go out the door"; most "chart a
course to the salad bar" and finish with mud pie.

Cheesecake Factory, The ◐ 🅢 | 18 | 17 | 16 | $18 |
Chevy Chase Pavilion, 5345 Wisconsin Ave., NW (bet.
Jennifer St. & Western Ave.), 202-364-0500
White Flint Mall, 11301 Rockville Pike (Nicholson Ln.),
Bethesda, MD, 301-770-0999
☑ The "best cheesecake ever" on a massively portioned,
"please-everyone" menu competes with noise, "stadium
ambiance", no reserving and "interminable waits" at
Chevy Chase's busiest restaurant; we doubt the summer
'94 opening of the unrated Bethesda location will shorten
your time in its holding pen.

Chesapeake Seafood Crab House 🅢 | 15 | 9 | 14 | $17 |
3607 Wilson Blvd. (bet. Nelson & Monroe Sts.), Arlington,
VA, 703-528-8888
☑ At this unassuming Clarenton Vietnamese with very
good food and "no decorating budget", the seafood is
available American style or, preferably, in unusual
Vietnamese soups and main dishes; outdoor seating on
the astroturf "patio is best" (ratings reflect confusion with
the similarly named American chain).

31

Chicken Place, The S
▽ 19 | 10 | 16 | $12
11201 Grandview Ave. (Reedie Dr.), Wheaton, MD,
301-946-1212

■ In Wheaton, this "tacky" but "terrific" Peruvian chicken griller is best known for its "moist", "well-seasoned" birds to take out or eat in; the staff is "very helpful" in describing such "down-to-earth" dishes as ocopa (potatoes with a peanut/cheese sauce) and there's weekend music.

China Canteen S
▽ 22 | 8 | 19 | $13
808 Hungerford Dr. (off Ivy League Ln.), Rockville, MD,
301-424-1606

■ "Everything tastes good" at this Rockville Cantonese where well-prepared, "unusual dishes" (check the board for daily specials), low prices and "soup-kitchen decor" lend a touch of "Chinatown authenticity"; locals also like the "good service", parking and home delivery.

China Chef S
20 | 15 | 17 | $15
11323 Georgia Ave. (University Blvd.), Wheaton, MD,
301-949-8170

■ It's no secret that this "homey mom-and-pop feeling" Wheaton storefront serves some of the "area's best Chinese food"; while virtually everything on the Cantonese menu is worth trying, surveyors single out the weekend dim sum as a best bet.

China Inn ◑ S
18 | 13 | 17 | $18
631 H St., NW (bet. 6th & 7th Sts.), 202-842-0909

◪ Although its modernized interior is looking "shabby" and service was never its strength, this Chinatown fixture is the source of some of the "best 'regular' Chinese food around" and its daily dim sum is "heaven"; critics consider it "uneven" and wonder why it's on our list.

"Ciao baby" Cucina S
18 | 21 | 18 | $26
Washington Sq., 1736 L St., NW (bet. 18th St. &
Connecticut Ave.), 202-331-1500

◪ An Americanized Italian that turned the defunct, but still handsome, 21 Federal into a happy-hour hot spot (with "free munchies"); twenty/thirtysomethings go "just to see the handsome waiters" and each other, or for "recruiting lunches" when the company's paying, but "most people know you don't go for the food."

Cities S
21 | 22 | 19 | $27
2424 18th St., NW (Columbia Rd.), 202-328-7194

◪ This "deconstructionist" original "stays fresh" by periodically changing its decor and menu to reflect a different region's food; one constant is real talent in the person of chef Mary Richter; try it for a romantic dinner, or "watch Adams Morgan wake up" at brunch.

CITRONELLE S 25 23 22 $42
The Latham Hotel, 3000 M St., NW (30th St.), 202-625-2150
■ Sitting near celebs ("Cronkite" one week, "then Ron Brown") vies with Michel Richard's French-accented California cuisine at this Georgetown "slice off" Citrus, his renowned LA restaurant; though the odd dish is a "lemon", most applaud Citronelle's "flashes of brilliance" and whimsy, its "classy" space, "well-trained" help and "relatively low" lunch prices.

City Lights of China S 23 14 19 $18
1731 Connecticut Ave., NW (bet. R & S Sts.), 202-265-6688
■ Lighting up its Dupont Circle neighborhood, the "best Chinese in city limits" woks out "better, fresher" versions of old "standbys", honors reservations, prices fairly and delivers "in a snowstorm"; eating in a "cramped" basement and being "rushed" are the trade-offs.

Clyde's ● S 17 19 18 $20
3236 M St., NW (Wisconsin Ave.), 202-333-9180
8332 Leesburg Pike (Rtes. 7 & 123), Vienna, VA, 703-734-1901
10221 Wincopin Circle (Rte. 175), Columbia, MD, 301-596-4050, (DC) 410-730-2829
Reston Town Ctr., Market St. (Reston Pkwy.), Reston, VA, 703-787-6601
☑ These "attractive", "lively" saloons capture the spirit of Washington, "yet each branch has its own touch"; all are virtually synonymous with burgers, bar food and brunch, but they are making a "serious attempt to lower prices" while upgrading their menus with "fresh produce."

Coco Loco S – – – M
810 7th St., NW (bet. H & I Sts.), 202-289-2626
Yannick Cam (ex Le Pavillon) and Savino Recine (Primi Piatti) got it all right at this sizzling South American – from the elegant "Mexican" tapas and all-you-can-eat Brazilian mixed grill to its new Downtown location, a soaring space filled with art and artifacts, gorgeous women, pols and Eurobods – not to mention the hot Brazilian dancers (don't touch) and musicians late at night.

COEUR DE LION S 24 26 25 $37
Henley Park Hotel, 926 Mass. Ave., NW (10th St.), 202-638-5200
■ Its new (since our last *Survey*) "young chef is learning" which means that the already "very good" Contemporary American food at this "romantic" Victorian hideaway near the Convention Center is likely to get better.

Collector, The [S] ▽ 14 17 15 $21
Dupont Plaza Hotel, 1500 New Hampshire Ave., NW (Dupont Circle), 202-797-0160
◪ A "highly commendable" concept – promoting "local art" – works well with "jazz and drinks" at this Dupont Circle hotel lounge and restaurant, but most "wish the (Eclectic) food was worthy of" what's on the walls; the $11.95 Sunday brunch is a good intro.

COLONNADE, THE [S] 23 25 23 $36
ANA Hotel, 2401 M St., NW (24th St.), 202-457-5000
■ This "elegant" and "capable" West End Contemporary American's many "winning ways" include a "romantic gazebo setting" and a "first-rate Sunday brunch"; however, it faces tough competition among hotel dining rooms.

Connaught Place [S] ▽ 24 21 23 $20
10425 North St. (Rte. 236 W. & University Dr.), Fairfax, VA, 703-352-5959
■ An "unusual location" in Fairfax City could explain why more reviewers haven't discovered this "charming" Indian; its "original" dishes, "light touch with oils" and polite, "helpful waiters" endear it to those who have.

COPPI'S RESTAURANT ◐ [S] 25 23 21 $15
1414 U St., NW (bet. 14th & 15th Sts.), 202-319-7773
■ High on our Bang for the Buck list, this "swell"-looking, brick-oven pizzeria had the crust to pioneer with gentrified toppings and salads in the "New U" area; now it's almost "impossible to get seated" on weekend nights.

Cottonwood Cafe [S] 20 20 19 $26
4844 Cordell Ave. (bet. Wisconsin Ave. & Old Georgetown Rd.), Bethesda, MD, 301-656-4844
◪ Despite "high-end" prices, "bad manners" and a "theme gone stale", this Bethesda "copycat" cowboy appeals to suburbanites looking for food "with fire and a Southwest twang" in "nice surroundings"; the bottom line: it's "always mobbed."

Coventry Cross [S] ▽ 18 15 18 $19
8401 Connecticut Ave. (Chevy Chase Lake Dr.), Chevy Chase, MD, 301-907-0368
◪ A "sorely needed" Chevy Chase "neighborhood pub" – and "a good one" – with "wonderful ale on tap" and "cheap English eats"; it's one of those places where the congenial "atmosphere makes up for all" its shortcomings; however, Anglo pub purists call it a "hoax."

Crisfield [S] 21 | 11 | 16 | $24

Lee Plaza, 8606 Colesville Rd. (Georgia Ave.), Silver Spring, MD, 301-588-1572
8012 Georgia Ave. (East-West Hwy. & Railroad St.), Silver Spring, MD, 301-589-1306 💳

◪ Past their "glory days", these "funky" Silver Spring fish houses preserve our "Maryland legacy" of crab imperial, stuffed shrimp, deep-fat frying and "salty servers"; critics cite "grumpy service in bus-station decor" and "less value."

Crisp & Juicy [S] 💳 21 | 3 | 14 | $9

Lee Heights Shopping Ctr., 4520 Lee Hwy. (Lorcom Ln.), Arlington, VA, 703-243-4222
Sunshine Sq. Shopping Ctr., 1331-G Rockville Pike, Rockville, MD, 301-251-8833
Leisure World Plaza, 3800 International Dr. (Georgia Ave.), Silver Spring, MD, 301-598-3333

■ Cheap "yummy food, crummy place" is the short of it; the rest is that these shopping-strip Latins produce "succulent" rotisserie chicken, charge less than you'd pay for the groceries and are "terrible places to eat in"; when you take out, "don't pass up the beans and rice."

Crystal Thai [S] 22 | 17 | 20 | $17

Arlington Forest Shopping Ctr., 4819 Arlington Blvd. (Park Dr.), Arlington, VA 703-522-1311

◪ "Homestyle" Thai in an Arlington strip mall that "concentrates on food" resulting in "exceptionally tasty" seafood but "spotty service"; locals feel "lucky" to have it as a neighbor, but some are unimpressed.

Da Domenico 20 | 17 | 20 | $27

1992 Chain Bridge Rd. (Rte. 123), McLean, VA, 703-790-9000

◪ "Dinner's not over till the fat man sings"; Dominic, the ebullient owner, is the life of a nightly party at this "old-fashioned" Tysons Corner Italian; he'll sing for your supper, but except for his "unrivaled" veal chop, the "uninspired" food and "outdated" decor can't keep tune with him.

D'Angelo [S] ▽ 20 | 20 | 19 | $22

4301 N. Fairfax Dr. (bet. Taylor & Utah Sts.), Arlington, VA 703-522-1800

◪ Mark Caraluzzi (Bistro/Bistro) offers an edible reminiscence of family-style Italo-American dining that's right in step with the '90s with its focus on health ("less fat and beef") and value ("'single' portions feed a family"); critics say its service and kitchen need to "refine a bit more."

Dante S   19 20 19 $26
*1148 Walker Rd. (Colvin Run Rd.), Great Falls, VA,
703-759-3131*
⬛ A "pleasant destination" serving "fine" (aka "pricey")
Northern Italian fare in "intimate" rooms; enough
surveyors mistook it for a U Street "post-show" stop that's
"popular with actors" and other "interesting" types to
make our ratings questionable but not out of the ballpark.

Dean & DeLuca Cafe   19 15 12 $13
3276 M St., NW (33rd St.), 202-342-2500 S
*1299 Pennsylvania Ave., NW (bet. 13th & E Sts.), 202-628-8155
1919 Pennsylvania Ave., NW (bet. 19th & Eye Sts.),
202-296-4327*
⬛ "Chic" streetside cafes where "small tastes" of NYC
(salads, sandwiches, simple entrees, coffee and desserts)
are served cafeteria style; they "add a stylish dimension
to casual DC dining", but for "NY prices" and "major lines."

Delhi Dhaba S   19 6 13 $11
*2424 Wilson Blvd. (bet. Barton St. & Clarendon Blvd.),
Arlington, VA, 703-524-0008
7236 Woodmont Ave. (bet. Bethesda Ave. & Elm St.),
Bethesda, MD, 301-718-0008*

Delhi Darbar S
8794-S Sacramento Dr. (Rte. 1), Alexandria, VA, 703-781-0009
⬛ "Do take out" unless you're in the mood for "Indian
'MTV'", school-lunchroom service and "grubbiness"
along with the "good, cheap" Indian food at these suburban
buffets; they're touted for "eating alone or with kids."

Dfouny S   ▽ 21 16 19 $21
*815 King St. (bet. Alfred & Columbus Sts.), Alexandria, VA,
703-549-3444*
⬛ "Appetizers are the appeal" at this "intimate" VA
Lebanese, "but that belly dancer" also charms; well-
priced Middle Eastern favorites, "tremendous portions"
and "eagerness to please" are what you'd expect in an
offshoot of the successful Lebanese Taverna; it's "perfect"
when you don't want to wear a tie.

Dixie Grill   14 17 14 $15
518 10th St., NW (bet. E & F Sts.), 202-628-4800
⬛ Deep in the "heart of touristville" (across from Ford's
Theatre), this ersatz Southern dive may be an entertaining
"place to play pool" and drink cheap beer, but many
consider the "greasy food" and "lackadaisical" service
nearly "bad enough to reignite the Civil War."

Donatello ◐ S   21 | 18 | 21 | $27
2514 L St., NW (Pennsylvania Ave.), 202-333-1485
☑ The "Maytag of Italian restaurants" – "steady and always available", this "woody West End townhouse" is a fixture for prix fixe, pre-/post-Kennedy Center dining; though "a little cramped" inside, it's "relaxed" for a meal on the sidewalk terrace.

Donna Adele S   20 | 19 | 19 | $33
2100 P St., NW (bet. 21st & 22nd Sts.), 202-296-1142
☑ Opinions of this "upscale" Northern Italian off Dupont Circle are decidedly mixed: "wonderful sidewalk dining", "at its best, it competes with the best", "great personal touch" vs. "overblown, overpriced, overrated" and "not in the Big League."

Duangrat's S   24 | 21 | 21 | $22
5878 Leesburg Pike (Glen Forest Rd.), Falls Church, VA, 703-820-5775
■ The area's top-rated Thai transforms an Arlington strip mall into a pretty "traditional setting" for "pungent", "delicate" food; "charming" costumed waitresses, ethnic dance performances (weekends) and dishes "unavailable elsewhere" come at way less cost than a French or Italian meal Downtown.

Dusit S   21 | 17 | 20 | $16
2404 University Blvd. W. (Georgia Ave.), Wheaton, MD, 301-949-4140
☑ "Prettier than most", this Wheaton neighborhood Thai is run by "nice people", priced right, and produces "hot and delicious" dishes ("especially curries"); dissenters, citing "assembly-line" "lukewarm, bland food" conclude "we've given up."

East Wind S   22 | 18 | 21 | $22
809 King St. (bet. Washington St. & Rte. 1), Alexandria, VA, 703-836-1515
☑ "Competitive", if a bit "faded", this "lovely, quiet" Vietnamese in Old Town has leveled off since changing hands a few years ago; however, reaction to its downscaled menu and "cheaper" tab ranges from "good buy, good food" to "once a favorite, now a loss."

Eat First S ⊄   – | – | – | I
728 7th St., NW (bet. G & H Sts.), 202-347-0936
Sinophiles who prize "eating first" give high marks to this Spartan Chinatown canteen – it's hard to go wrong with anything on the extensive English and Chinese menus, but we hear that the Hong Kong dishes guarantee repeat visits.

Ecco Cafe S
|20| |17| |18| |$19|

220 N. Lee St. (Cameron St.), Alexandria, VA, 703-684-0321
☑ Diana Damewood, a "great hostess", turns what looks
like another "pre-packaged" pizza and pasta place into
one of Old Town's "liveliest" Friday nights; go for "decent
Italian eats" at a "good price" and "ask for half portions"
from a staff that "does it with a smile."

El Caribe S
|19| |16| |18| |$22|

3288 M St., NW (bet. Potomac & 32nd Sts.), 202-338-3121
8130 Wisconsin Ave. (bet. Cordell Ave. & Battery Ln.),
Bethesda, MD, 301-656-0888
☑ Latin standbys with an "extensive" menu of "hearty" fare,
"elbow-to-elbow" ethnicity (Georgetown), "fireplace" charm
(Bethesda) and waiters with a sense of humor as salty as
the margaritas; go early for food, late for "atmosphere."

El Tamarindo ● S
|18| |8| |15| |$13|

1785 Florida Ave., NW (bet. 18th & U Sts.), 202-328-3660
4910 Wisconsin Ave., NW (42nd St.), 202-244-8888
7331 Georgia Ave., NW (Fessenden Rd.), 202-291-0525
☑ Favored by "starving students" and families with kids,
these Salvadorans dish up massive platters of cheap,
"honest" food that "actually tastes good"; the help is short
on English but not on good will, and the premises "dingy"
to put it mildly; after 11 PM, they "really get interesting."

Elysium S
|–| |–| |–| |E|

(fka Morrison House Grill)
Morrison House Hotel, 116 S. Alfred St. (bet. King &
Prince Sts.), Alexandria, VA, 703-838-8000
A "ritzy", "small hotel" dining room in Old Town known for
its classy "European" style; its new name signals its new
culinary orientation towards Mediterranean-accented
Contemporary American food – happily, the cosseting
hasn't changed.

Enriqueta's S
|21| |16| |19| |$20|

2811 M St., NW (bet. 28th & 29th Sts.), 202-338-7772
☑ This festive-looking, Georgetown cantina is respected
for its "authentic" Mexican food that goes "beyond tacos"
to the moles and seafood dishes popularized by the movie
Like Water for Chocolate; neither the uncomfortable
seating nor the "mysteriously quick" delivery get high marks.

Evans Farm Inn S
|13| |19| |16| |$23|

1696 Chain Bridge Rd. (Rte. 123), McLean, VA, 703-356-8000
☑ A colonial-theme "family place" with 40 acres of
bucolic things "to do"; it generates plenty of traffic as
well as perennial gripes about the kitsch, the kitchen and
kindergarten help; efforts to upgrade the "Sitting Duck
Pub" are said to be paying off.

Eye Street Cafe   21 | 17 | 19 | $17
1915 I St., NW (bet. 19th & 20th Sts.), 202-457-0773
■ "You feel enthusiasm" from the staff as well as the
customers at this "great 'little' restaurant'" in the K Street
corridor; perfect for a "modest lunch", its standout pizzas
and casual Mediterranean choices draw midday lines;
ergo, dinner may be "the real treat."

Faccia Luna Pizzeria S ⌷   20 | 15 | 17 | $15
2400 Wisconsin Ave., NW (Calvert St.), 202-337-3132
2909 Wilson Blvd. (Filmore St.), Arlington, VA, 703-276-3099
☑ "Don't expect the moon", but if you're searching for that
"elusive holy grail – decent pizza", these local parlors are
worth a try; along with "fresh toppings" and crispy crusts,
you'll find salads, hoagies, pastas, "good music" and
interesting beers, but not much decor "unless you play pool."

Falls Landing S   21 | 20 | 21 | $30
Village Ctr., 774 Walker Rd., Great Falls, VA, 703-759-4650
☑ A "fallback" for suburban celebrations, this "well-run",
genteel Virginian serves "predictably excellent" seafood
in a colonial setting "your grandparents" will love; fault-
finders term it "stodgy."

Fedora Cafe S   18 | 18 | 17 | $22
8521 Leesburg Pike (bet. Rte. 123 & Dulles Access Rd.),
Tysons Corner, VA, 703-556-0100
☑ If you live or work in Tysons Corner, this '90s fern bar is
a "good place to network" and "not a bad place to dine"
with its trendy menu of Italian-accented "almost fast
food"; however, the "patchy" food, service and vibes are
definitely "outside the Beltway."

Fern Street Bistro S   – | – | – | M
Burke Ctr., 6025A Burke Centre Pkwy. (corner of Burke
Commons), Burke, VA, 703-425-9463
One of the "best restaurants no one's ever heard of", say
write-ins who are jubilant about the reopening of this smart-
looking, creative Eclectic wine bar/cafe in the culinary
hinterlands beyond Fairfax – this one is worth the trip.

Fes S   ▽ 19 | 22 | 20 | $29
4917 Elm St. (bet. Arlington Blvd. & Woodmont Ave.),
Bethesda, MD, 301-718-1777
☑ Reviews of the Moroccan "evening's entertainment" at
this Bethesda storefront range from praise for "huge
helpings" of "excellent, authentic dishes" to protests that
"even the belly dancer was limpid"; only fixed-price,
multicourse dinners are served at night, but you can audition
the food (not the dancer) at the "great buy" lunch buffet.

Filomena Ristorante S   20 | 18 | 18 | $27
1063 Wisconsin Ave., NW (bet. M & K Sts.), 202-337-2782
This is the "dark", "overcrowded", "chaotic",
gastronomically incorrect ("fill your face") Italian in
Georgetown where Messrs. Clinton and Kohl downed a
mega-calorie lunch that sparked such quips as: "site of
the tortellini summit"; but hey, lots of others love it too.

Firehook Bakery   23 | 13 | 17 | $10
and Coffeehouse S
106 N. Lee St. (bet. King & Cameron Sts.), Alexandria, VA,
703-519-8020
The "hearty" artisan bread at this Old Town bakery/
cafe is a "meal in itself", and the "superb" pastries epitomize
dessert; however, customers can also forage at the
"gourmet" shop next door for sandwich fillers and salads,
and enjoy the "coffeehouse atmosphere" with live music
and poetry readings.

Fleetwood's ◑ S   – | – | – | M
44 Canal Ctr. Plaza (N. Fairfax Circle), Alexandria, VA,
703-548-6425
Mick Fleetwood's new restaurant/blues club in Alexandria
features a Contemporary American pizza, pasta and grill
menu, state-of-the-art acoustics, an industrial-modern
layout that gives nearly every seat a performance view
and the nicest riverside patio in town; it books some of
Mick's high-profile friends as acts but no reserving means
go very, very early.

Florida Ave. Grill S   17 | 10 | 15 | $12
1100 Florida Ave., NW (11th St.), 202-265-1586
A soulful Saturday morning breakfast at this "no-
nonsense" Downtown Southern dive is the artery-clogging
antidote to cravings for grits, greens and gravy – they "still
do it in the same old way" – with a "capital 'G' for grease."

Foggy Bottom Cafe S   19 | 17 | 18 | $23
River Inn, 924 25th St., NW (bet I & K Sts.), 202-338-8707
"There's something very comfortable" about this simple
restaurant in Foggy Bottom that adds value to its "well-
cooked" American food and "pleasant" manners; "location"
isn't the only reason why it's a "Kennedy Center favorite."

Food Factory S ⊭   21 | 4 | 10 | $10
4221 N. Fairfax Dr. (Glebe Rd.), Arlington, VA, 703-527-2279
"Cheap eats" don't get much cheaper, better or more
basic than at this Ballston Pakistani where the "succulent
kebabs", nan bread, vegetable curries and "school
cafeteria" mayhem remind one of "eating out in Peshawar."

Foong Lin [S] | 19 | 12 | 19 | $17 |

7710 Norfolk Ave. (Fairmont Ave.), Bethesda, MD, 301-656-3427

■ "People love" this "traditional red" suburban Chinese cliche because it treats them "like old friends", serves their favorite dishes and is a "buy" at lunch – "boring", but "you'll never have an empty water glass."

Fortune [S] | 22 | 14 | 17 | $18 |

Greenforest Shopping Ctr., 5900 Leesburg Pike (Bailey's Crossroads), Falls Church, VA, 703-998-8888
North Point Village Ctr., 1428 Reston Pkwy. (bet. Rte. 7 & Baron Cameron Rd.), Reston, VA, 703-318-8898

◪ The "awesome" parade of dim sum carts and "daunting" seafood menu at this Cantonese bargain banquet hall in Bailey's Crossroads (and its fledgling in Reston) are as close as DC gets "to Hong Kong"; but the "impersonal, atmosphere" feels more like the People's Republic of China.

Four and Twenty Blackbirds [S] | – | – | – | M |

Route 522 (Rte. 647), Flint Hill, VA, 703-675-1111

A drive to "God's country" (in Rappahanock, VA) and a bit of "small village" life ("get there before church lets out") whet the appetite for the "innovative", internationally-inspired, but local-ingredient-based, New American cuisine served in this "charming" converted country store; be sure to reserve upstairs.

Four Rivers [S] | 19 | 9 | 16 | $15 |

184 Rollins Ave. (E. Jefferson St.), Rockville, MD, 301-230-2900

■ Though this "unpretentious", "inexpensive" Rockville storefront woks out "satisfying" Szechuan standards, "the best things" – "unusual Taiwanese dishes" found "nowhere else" – "are on the Chinese menu" or just ask your waiter about "the daily specials."

Frog and the Redneck, The ▽ | 26 | 22 | 24 | $31 |

1423 E. Cary St. (bet. 14th & 15th Sts.), Richmond, VA, 804-648-FROG

■ The "redneck" is chef Jimmy Sneed, but as far as we know the only "frog" is Jean-Louis Palladin, Jimmy's mentor who drops in occasionally to stir the pot; it's "worth going" the hundred miles to Richmond to taste the "amazing" things Jimmy does with regional products in his "fun and funky" establishment.

Full Kee ◑ S | 20 | 6 | 14 | $13 |
509 H St., NW (bet. 5th & 6th Sts.), 202-371-2233
Full Key ◑ S
*Wheaton Manor Shopping Ctr., 2227 University Blvd. W.
(Georgia Ave.), Wheaton, MD, 301-933-8388*
■ These "specialists" in the meal-sized soups and noodle
dishes of Hong Kong "look like nothing" and don't win
hospitality awards but "you can't beat the price, or the
congee" at either location; separately managed, Wheaton
is more "comfortable", Chinatown more "fun."

Gabriel S   ∇ | 19 | 19 | 20 | $28 |
*Radisson-Barceló Washington Hotel, 2121 P St., NW (bet.
21st & 22nd Sts.), 202-956-6690*
◪ A "real promising" newcomer in handsomely redecorated
Dupont Circle West space with an "up-to-the-minute menu"
of Southwest-influenced tapas and "fusion" entrees; it's
still early, but yeas outnumber nays — with loud hurrays
for "late hours" and "light fare" at the bar.

Gaby's | 21 | 19 | 20 | $36 |
3311 Connecticut Ave., NW (Macomb St.), 202-364-8909
◪ Great expectations when Gaby (ex La Brasserie) took
over this "treasured" Cleveland Park French bistro collided
with a "shaky start"; as he settles in, there's "plenty of
déjà vu" on the menu (some nights "beautifully executed",
sometimes not), but fortunately the word is: "improving."

GALILEO S | 26 | 23 | 23 | $44 |
1110 21st St., NW (bet. L & M Sts.), 202-293-7191
■ Widely recognized as DC's premiere Italian, Roberto
Donna's Northern "classic" was also voted No. 3 in overall
popularity in this year's *Survey*; a meal here is a "very
special dining experience" with "wonderful food" enhanced
by caring staff; some of the best tables are in the kitchen
where you may want to arrange a "taste-everything dinner."

Gangplank S | 15 | 18 | 16 | $24 |
600 Water St., SW (7th St. & Maine Ave.), 202-554-5000
◪ A beacon in the Maine Avenue "nautical nightmare"
that attracts Arena Stage ticketholders, tourists and
romantics looking for a sunset view with good parking;
drinks and crab cakes on the floating deck are a safe bet,
but the seafood menu can produce many a "happy
surprise" and insiders say everything gets "better much
later" at night.

Garden Cafe S   ▽ 22 | 17 | 21 | $26
*State Plaza Hotel, 2116 F St., NW (bet. 21st & 22nd Sts.),
202-861-0331*
■ Last year, this Foggy Bottom hotel dining room delighted
discriminating State Department and GWU diners by
hiring some "innovative" chefs (most recently Richard
and Lynn Mahan, ex Oliver's) and now, even though the
cheerily modern interior isn't "quite up to the style" of the
Contemporary American food, the secluded courtyard and
"attentive staff" can make any meal an occasion.

Gary's   19 | 18 | 20 | $30
1800 M St., NW (18th St.), 202-463-6470
☑ One of the few remaining "men-meet-meat" restaurants,
this "clubby" Downtown steakhouse is still a midday "haunt"
of "big eaters" with deep pockets; but with Duke's doors
shut and many people eating "line-of-duty" lunches in their
firm's dining rooms, Gary's may "need a wake-up" call.

Generous George's Positive   18 | 15 | 16 | $13
Pizza & Pasta Place S
*3006 Duke St. (Roth St.), Alexandria, VA, 703-370-4303 ◗
Concord Shopping Ctr., 6131 Backlick Rd. (Commerce St.),
Springfield, VA, 703-451-7111
7031 Little River Tpke. (John Marr Dr.), Annandale, VA,
703-941-9600*
☑ These highly original pizza palaces feature "cheap",
"thick, chewy" mega-pizzas loaded with "every topping
imaginable", "gaudy" kid-proofed settings and a positive
pasta pie (pizza plus pasta) that makes even hungry teens
cry 'uncle'; still, a few complain: "a lot of bad is still bad."

Georgetown Bar & Grill ◗ S   ▽ 17 | 16 | 16 | $21
*The Georgetown Inn, 1310 Wisconsin Ave., NW (N St.),
202-333-8900*
☑ Oddly enough, this comfortable "clubby" retreat – with
free on-site parking in the heart of Georgetown – hasn't
caught on, possibly because the American kitchen is still
"trying to find its identity" (currently opting for familiar
sandwiches, seafood and light entrees) and the staff
hasn't turned on.

Georgetown Seafood Grill, The S   19 | 13 | 17 | $24
3063 M St., NW (bet. 30th & 31st Sts.), 202-333-7038
☑ Georgetown regulars drop by this "no-fuss" fish house
for "oysters and a Sauvignon Blanc" on Saturday afternoon,
while tourists "overcrowd" the old wooden booths and
raw bar at night; it's "fine" for "good plain seafood", if you
"don't push it."

Georgia Brown's S
21 | 22 | 20 | $28

950 15th St., NW (K St.), 202-393-4499

■ At this luminous power station, "displaced" Southerners sell displaced Northerners and Westerners on grits, greens, fried chicken and all that "rich, unhealthy, greasy but so good" stuff, in a gussied-up Adam Tihany–designed setting; it has well-spaced tables, a staff that "knows its stuff" and is near the White House.

Geppetto S
19 | 15 | 16 | $17

2917 M St., NW (bet. 29th & 30th Sts.), 202-333-2602
Wildwood Shopping Ctr., 10257 Old Georgetown Rd.
(Democracy Blvd.), Bethesda, MD, 301-493-9230

◩ Cheesy, cheeseless or "packed" with pepperoni, "pig out" on pizza at these cutesy "family places" and you won't eat for a week; sure, they offer salads, "healthy" pies and "lighter choices", but it's the pizza that generates the "agonizing" waits.

Geranio S
22 | 20 | 20 | $27

722 King St. (bet. Washington & Columbus Sts.),
Alexandria, VA, 703-548-0088

◩ "Sometimes overlooked", but not by Alexandria old-timers who tell us that seafood and pasta are "done well" at this "cozy", conventional Italian and that the "boss watches out for you"; a distinct minority are "not impressed" and warn that the early seating is rushed.

GERARD'S PLACE
24 | 21 | 22 | $44

915 15th St., NW (McPherson Sq.), 202-737-4445

■ At Gerard Pangaud's "very Parisian" Downtown place, subdued appointments keep the focus on his gutsy and "rewarding" haute bourgeois French cuisine; "when he's on" (usually), it's easy to dismiss "overbooking" and "cramped" seating; Monday night is a "must" for wine buffs – the corkage charge is waived.

Germaine's S
22 | 19 | 20 | $30

2400 Wisconsin Ave., NW (Calvert St.), 202-965-1185

◩ A pan-Asian pioneer, whose "distinctive" food and "relaxing" charm is legendary; her Upper Georgetown dining room feels "like Saigon before the French left" (i.e. it could use a "face-lift") but also because it's loaded with "literary (media) types."

Ginza's
∇ 21 | 16 | 21 | $25

1009 21st St., NW (bet. K & L Sts.), 202-833-1244

■ At this midtown Japanese, the sushi is fresh and well-made and the cooked dishes, fulfilling; the fact that the setting is "too plain for social dining" suits those Tokyo business suits just fine.

Good Fortune [S] ◐ 20 | 13 | 15 | $15
2646 University Blvd. (bet. Viers Mill Rd. & Georgia Ave.), Wheaton, MD, 301-929-8818
■ "Dim sum" is a major draw at this "ordinary" looking Wheaton Chinese, yet it would be a pity not to try the "wide variety" of regular Cantonese selections; of course, the place has its "off nights", but you can't do much better than its "usually excellent" and well-priced food.

Grill from Ipanema, The ◐ [S] 20 | 21 | 19 | $23
1858 Columbia Rd., NW (Belmont Rd.), 202-986-0757
◩ "Strong drinks" and "attitude" set the tone at this Adams Morgan hot spot where "chic" lovelies who "can't believe Brazilian women eat that heavy stuff" (feijoada, moqueca) display themselves against the "black-on-black" decor.

Grill, The [S] 23 | 25 | 23 | $36
Ritz-Carlton at Pentagon City, 1250 South Hayes St. (bet. 15th St. & Army Navy Dr.), Arlington, VA, 703-415-5000
■ Having lunch in this "peaceful" contemporary hotel dining room is "like taking a mini-vacation in the middle of the day"; you "feel pampered" in such "beautiful surroundings" and everything from Châteaubriand to burgers tastes "great"; it's also a "surefire business setting" offering "elegant breakfasts", dinners and teas.

Guards, The [S] 17 | 18 | 18 | $26
2915 M St. (bet. 29th & 30th Sts.), 202-965-2350
◩ An "atmospheric" watering hole for "aging yuppies", this is where Georgetown "bar people" end the night; while still capable of producing the "roaring fire, great hospitality and splendid food" (steaks, chops, fish, burgers and salads) of the "old days", it (and its clientele) are getting "tired."

Gulf Coast Kitchen [S] – | – | – | I
7750 Woodmont Ave. (bet. Cheltenham Dr. & Old Georgetown Rd.), Bethesda, MD, 301-652-6278
Some of the laid-back allure of Key West beckons Bethesda twentysomethings to this roomy roadhouse replica, where rooftop seating, breezy manners and a hokey menu of sandwiches, hefty salads, and "Southern comfort" plates provide a trendy substitute for the real thing.

Haandi [S] 24 | 19 | 22 | $21
Falls Plaza Shopping Ctr., 1222 W. Broad St. (Rte. 7), Falls Church, VA, 703-533-3501
4904 Fairmont Ave. (Old Georgetown Rd.), Bethesda, MD, 301-718-0121
■ These suburban subcontinentals get "high marks" for "first-rate tandoori", breads, "family-friendly" spicing and "pleasant atmosphere"; they're "a good deal", as weekend crowds attest, and very handy for "out-of-town guests."

Hamburger Hamlet [S] 16 | 15 | 16 | $15

3125 M St., NW (bet. Wisconsin Ave. & 31st St.), 202-965-6970
5225 Wisconsin Ave., NW (Jennifer St.), 202-244-2038
10400 Old Georgetown Rd. (Democracy Blvd.), Bethesda, MD, 301-897-5350
Crystal City Underground, 1601 Crystal Sq. Arcade, Crystal City, VA, 703-413-0422
Rio at Washington Ctr., 9811 Washingtonian Blvd., Gaithersburg, MD, 301-417-0773
1700 N. Beauregard St. (Seminary Rd.), Alexandria, VA, 703-998-1112

◪ These "prototypical fern bars" are the "chain to pull" when "burger hunger" hits or the kids want the "same old, same old" burger, fries and a shake; their "formula works" – to a point; waits, crowds and crayons come with the territory.

Hard Rock Cafe [S] 14 | 20 | 15 | $16

999 E St., NW (10th St.), 202-737-ROCK

◪ A must for anyone with kids, yet grown-ups also use the Downtown HRC to "escape from a busy workday" or "hang out" until nearby clubs rev up; rock 'n' roll relics, "decent" burgers, "reasonable prices", "perky" servers and that loud beat explain why; crowds and noise explain why not.

Hard Times Cafe [S] 19 | 15 | 17 | $12

Woodley Gardens Shopping Ctr., 1117 Nelson St. (Rte. 28), Rockville, MD, 301-294-9720
1404 King St. (West St.), Alexandria, VA, 703-683-5340
3028 Wilson Blvd. (Highland St.), Arlington, VA 703-528-2233
K-Mart Shopping Ctr., 394 Elden St. (bet. Herndon Pkwy. & Van Buren St.), Herndon, VA, 703-318-8941

◪ Aka "Heartburn City", these "down 'n' dirty" chili parlors are "great, if you were raised that way", i.e. on "good cheap chili any way you want it" and "great cornbread"; but "talk about grease" – "if John Belushi were alive, this is where there'd be a food fight."

Havana Cafe [S] (fka La Cantinita) – | – | – | M

3100 Clarendon Blvd. (Washington Blvd.), Arlington, VA, 703-524-3611

The "character and grace" of old Havana is recreated in this vibrant Clarendon cafe where such fine, "authentic" dishes as roast pork or red snapper vinaigrette at popular prices earn respect for an often underrated cuisine.

Head's 15 | 11 | 14 | $15

400 First St., SE (D St.), 202-546-4545

◪ Maybe this Hill hangout is merely shoulders "above the average BBQ" joint, but given its prime House-side location, they could serve smoked anything and still pack the place with "cheapskate lobbyists" and staffers; it "desperately needs trained servers", not would-be staffers.

Herb's ● ⬛ S   – | – | – | M

Governor's House Holiday Inn, 1615 Rhode Island Ave., NW (17th St.), 202-333-4372

A "funky combo" of Midwesterners, local literati and theater people find their way to this renovated Holiday Inn near Thomas Circle – the former on account of its location and outdoor patio, the latter drawn by its owner, arts patron Herb White; while the basic American food won't win any awards, it's a "very good value, particularly lunch."

Hibiscus Cafe S   21 | 23 | 19 | $24

3401 K St. (34th St.), 202-338-0408

⬛ For "imaginative" island food, try this "lively" hip hop" spot in Georgetown ("hidden under the Whitehurst Freeway where the tourists can't find it"); "every detail" of the "electric bright" setting "catches your eye", but a more serious question is – can you catch the waiter's eye?

Hinode S   19 | 17 | 19 | $20

Bethesda Shopping Ctr., 4914 Hampden Ln. (Arlington Rd.), Bethesda, MD, 301-654-0908

☑ One of many "neighborhood Japanese" cafes providing healthy, affordable "fast food" in the burbs; at this dining level, if the "sushi is fresh and the tempura is light" (as it usually is here), and the help is "pleasant" and nice to kids, no one cares about the refinements.

Hisago S   24 | 23 | 22 | $36

3050 K St., NW (Washington Harbour), 202-944-4181

☑ A "typical tab" at this Japanese import "resembles the trade deficit", yet if you have the yen (and can negotiate "the Japanese menu"), it has "exquisite" sushi in an "elegant" Washington Harbour setting; we hear rumors that prices are dropping – it got "too expensive even for the Japanese."

Hogate's S   12 | 14 | 13 | $22

800 Water St., SW (bet. 9th St. & Maine Ave.), 202-484-6300

☑ Locals love to trash this Maine Avenue mass feedery; but go nonetheless "for the jazz and view", "networking", pre–Arena Stage or for rum buns at brunch; on the culinary side, one of our *Survey*'s lowest food ratings speaks for itself.

Houlihan's S   14 | 14 | 15 | $16

4444 Willard Ave. (Western Ave.), Chevy Chase, MD, 301-654-9020
6900 Old Keene Mill Rd. (Backlick Rd.), Springfield, VA, 703-451-0662

⬛ "Predictable and cheap", these convenient synthetic pubs are geared for "family eating" ("burgers and things"), "nourishment while shopping", "brunch on a budget" or a simple business lunch; at night, they're packed with sundowners trying to ride the "Blue Whale."

House of Chinese Gourmet S   18 | 12 | 15 | $17
*1485 Rockville Pike (1 block north of Congressional Plaza),
Rockville, MD, 301-984-9440*
☑ Known for its Peking duck special ("an excellent value")
and many "vegetarian possibilities" ("all good"), this
Rockville Pike "mainstay" brings a "serious" dimension to
"neighborhood Chinese" — making scattered negative
reports about food and "go-either-way" service negligible.

Houston's S   20 | 18 | 19 | $18
1065 Wisconsin Ave., NW (M St.), 202-338-7760 ●
*7715 Woodmont Ave. (bet. Cheltenham Dr. & Old
Georgetown Rd.),Bethesda, MD, 301-656-9755
12256 Rockville Pike (Montrose Rd.), Rockville, MD,
301-468-3535*
☑ Egalitarian rib and burger bars (everyone waits) with the
"best" burgers, ribs, salads, atmosphere and staff of any
restaurant in its class; but "is it worth waiting hours for?"

Hsiang Foong S   ▽ 18 | 11 | 17 | $15
*2919 N. Washington Blvd. (bet. Filmore & Garfield Sts.),
Arlington, VA, 703-522-1121*
☑ Still "serviceable", with a few "very good dishes" like the
tea-smoked duck and soups, but most of the food at this
Arlington Chinese isn't up to the "competition"; possibly
the well-meaning but "forgetful" staff are "losing interest."

Hunan Chinatown S   21 | 16 | 19 | $19
624 H St., NW (bet. 6th & 7th Sts.), 202-783-5858
☑ "One of Chinatown's best" sets the pace for "light-on-oil"
Szechuan and Hunan classics, and offers "standout" service
plus classy special events.

Hunan Lion S   20 | 18 | 19 | $22
*2070 Chain Bridge Rd. (Old Courthouse Rd.), Vienna, VA,
703-734-9828*

Hunan Lion II
*18140 The Galleria (near Tysons II), Tysons Corner, VA,
703-883-1938*
☑ Often lionized for "elegant", "affordable" entertaining,
a slide in ratings signals that these classy Tysons Corner
Chinese are now "unpredictable" — sometimes producing
"excellent, traditional" meals, sometimes "badly prepared"
and "rushed"; your odds improve with its dim sum lunch.

Hunan Manor S   – | – | – | M
*7091 Deepage Dr. (Carved Stone Rd.), Columbia, MD,
410-381-1134*
"Comfortable", "crowded" and "consistent", our Columbia
surveyors can't say enough nice things about their local
Chinese and its ability to satisfy a range of taste buds and
dining needs; try the "crispy beef or eggplant."

Hunan Number One ◑ S   21 │ 16 │ 19 │ $18
3033 Wilson Blvd. (Garfield St.), Arlington, VA, 703-528-1177
■ "Excellent" dim sum and Hong Kong–style dishes are
the "reason to visit" this Northern VA "favorite", although
"everything else" on its "diverse" menu is "good too"; it's
cheap, open late, and even the "atmosphere is ok."

Ichiban S   ▽ 20 │ 18 │ 19 │ $19
637 N. Frederick Ave. (near Lake Forest Mall),
Gaithersburg, MD, 301-670-0560
◪ A "suburban outpost" locally favored for its sushi,
tabletop Korean BBQ and commodious quarters, it's near
Gaithersburg where places that can handle groups are
still in short supply and even "so-so sushi" is a go go.

Il Cigno S   ▽ 21 │ 21 │ 20 │ $27
Lake Anne Plaza, 1617 Washington Plaza, Reston, VA,
703-471-0121
◪ "Terrific on a summer night", when Lake Anne breezes
and the staff's "personal touch" make this Reston Northern
Italian special; in winter, its "Downtown pretense" and
prices are more apparent.

Il Forno S   20 │ 10 │ 16 │ $13
4926 Cordell Ave. (bet. Old Georgetown & Norfolk Rds.),
Bethesda, MD, 301-652-7757
8941 N. Westland Dr. (Rte. 355), Gaithersburg, MD,
301-977-5900
◪ "When the basil is fresh", the crust is crisp and the
weather is nice enough to eat on the patio, this pizza stall
offers one of best cheap meals in Bethesda; otherwise,
it's strictly carry-out since it's overbright and loud inside;
some say the Gaithersburg branch "just doesn't have it."

Il Pizzico   23 │ 15 │ 21 │ $17
Suburban Park, 15209 Frederick Rd. (Gude Dr.), Rockville,
MD, 301-309-0610
■ Rapid expansion hasn't diluted the "great value", made
the staff less "accommodating", or diminished the lines (no
reserving) at this Italian expatriate; it's quite a trick to keep
prices for "fresh" tasting pasta at $6.95 and main courses
under $10 – here the trade-off is in portion size and decor.

Il Radicchio ◑ S   21 │ 18 │ 18 │ $19
1509 17th St., NW (bet. P & Q Sts.), 202-986-BOBS
■ At Roberto Donna's whimsically decorated 17th Street
spaghetteria, young urbans "scarf" bottomless bowls of
spaghetti ($6) sauced to suit ($1-$4), "pizza extraordinaire"
and "comfort-food" specials for $10 or less; their major
complaint is that it's "impossible to get in"; N.B. it's cloning
in Georgetown in early '95.

49

I Matti [S] | 23 | 19 | 19 | $28

2436 18th St., NW (bet. Belmont & Columbia Rds.), 202-462-8844

■ This high-energy trattoria dominates Adams Morgan dining with earthy pastas, original pizzas, "beautiful" salads and regional dishes; it's also a major "late-night" scene, and, since its post-*Survey* "face-lift", seems even more cosmopolitan (and less "cramped"); to avoid "the pressing mob" and waits, go for lunch.

Imperial Hotel Restaurant [S] ▽ | 25 | 24 | 22 | $39

The Imperial Hotel, 208 High St. (Cross St.), Chestertown, MD, 410-778-5000

See Baltimore Alphabetical Directory.

Inn at Glen Echo [S] | 19 | 20 | 19 | $25

6119 Tulane Ave. (MacArthur Blvd. & Cabin John Pkwy.), Glen Echo, MD, 301-229-2280

◪ An "ordinary" (in every sense of the word) with extraordinary surroundings overlooking Glen Echo Park; despite "serious" efforts to transform this former roadhouse into a credible modern American restaurant, it's best for a "relaxed" brunch or a "romantic" dinner on the deck.

INN AT LITTLE WASHINGTON, THE [S] | 29 | 28 | 28 | $68

The Inn at Little Washington, Middle & Main Sts., Washington, VA, 703-675-3800

■ There are "not enough stars or diamonds or pips or toques or anything" to describe this "dreamy" inn in the Virginia countryside (No. 1 in this *Survey*) where chef/co-owner Patrick O'Connell's world-class modern American food, "romantic" surroundings and the "attention paid to each detail" create "an experience you'll never forget"; stay overnight and wake up to the best breakfast of your life.

INN AT PERRY CABIN, THE [S] | 24 | 26 | 24 | $47

The Inn at Perry Cabin, 308 Watkins Ln. (Talbot St.), St. Michaels, MD, 410-745-2200

See Baltimore Alphabetical Directory.

I RICCHI | 24 | 23 | 22 | $40

1220 19th St., NW (bet. M & N Sts.), 202-835-0459

◪ Like a "Ferrari", this Northern Italian can be a "stellar performer", has a "functional" design and a "powerhouse" clientele under its hood; its robust Tuscan cooking "proves good food doesn't have to be fancy or sauced", but without "the right waiter", the service "borders on being an actionable offense"; in short, not everyone can handle it.

Iron Gate S   17 | 21 | 18 | $23
1734 N St., NW (bet. 17th & 18th Sts.), 202-737-1370
◪ It can be "worth sacrificing food" for in-town ambiance in an arbored courtyard or fireside, but what a pity that this Dupont Circle carriage house can't do both; its staff and Mediterranean cooking are chancy and unless you're near the hearth, "inside is pretty grim."

Ivy's Place S   18 | 9 | 17 | $15
3520 Connecticut Ave., NW (Porter St.), 202-363-7802
7929 Norfolk Ave. (Cordell Ave.), Bethesda, MD, 301-654-6444
◪ Low-budget storefronts whose Indonesian-Thai "home cooking" will "clear your sinuses" without emptying your wallet; Cleveland Park's sidewalk tables plug diners into an eclectic street scene; most find "Bethesda dull."

Jade Palace S   18 | 15 | 18 | $17
Woodmont Corner, 7708 Woodmont Ave. (Old Georgetown Rd.), Bethesda, MD, 301-657-1624
◪ Prized for "once-a-week" family dining in Bethesda and for using "fresh ideas and fresh ingredients" in its "standard Chinese food"; this suburbanite is neither a gem nor a palace, but it's "reliable", "attractive" and "well-priced."

Jaimalito's S   15 | 18 | 15 | $19
Washington Harbour, 3000 K St., NW, 202-944-4400
◪ Celebrating Friday night summer madness on the Potomac, the youthful "overflow from Sequoia" spills onto the stretch of Washington Harbour's fountain plaza staked out by this Tex-Mexican; most choose to "stay with drinks" rather than pay a "premium" for "nothing special" food and a staff "taking siestas."

Jaleo ◐ S   23 | 22 | 19 | $23
480 Seventh St. NW (E St.), 202-628-7949
■ Credit this wildly successful Spaniard for jump starting the tapas craze with its "sophisticated" small plates (plus some rustic entrees); at the same time it has "raised property values" drawing a mix of art, theater and government to its "trend-setting" digs in the New Downtown; "bring the crowd", but note, there's no prime-time reserving.

JEAN-LOUIS   27 | 24 | 26 | $64
The Watergate Hotel, 2650 Virginia Ave., NW (New Hampshire Ave.), 202-298-4488
■ "Justly famous", Jean-Louis Palladin's elegant yet surprisingly "relaxing" Watergate boutique is a magnet for visiting "connoisseurs" ("best in the city" in our *Survey*); let him "dazzle" you with a "tasting menu" composed daily from custom-grown products or with his pre-theater dinner, a $45 "steal"; upstairs, his bistro Palladin has less sculpted plates and more sculpted prices.

Jean-Michel S   22 | 20 | 21 | $34
Wildwood Shopping Ctr., 10223 Old Georgetown Rd.
(Democracy Blvd.), Bethesda, MD, 301-564-4910
■ A combo of "fine" French dining, suburban parking and
the personal touch of the king of K Street pampering,
Jean-Michel Farret, accounts for the instant success of
this Wildwood "shopping center" sell-out; even if a "safe"
menu and "retro '60s" decor are "not worth a trip from
Downtown", it proves that not having to leave the
neighborhood is what matters.

Jefferson Restaurant, The S   24 | 24 | 24 | $41
Jefferson Hotel, 1200 16th St., NW (M St.), 202-833-6206
☑ There's "always something interesting" on the
Contemporary American menu at this "intimate" Downtown
dining room, yet many "forget to go", perhaps because of its
"too too Republican" Bush-era associations, or because
the "price for chef Will Greenwood's experimentation" is
that it's "not always on"; try it for an "elegant" brunch.

Jockey Club, The S   23 | 24 | 23 | $43
Ritz-Carlton Hotel, 2100 Mass. Ave., NW (21st St.),
202-659-8000.
■ The successful renovation of DC's "21" Club – thank
God "they made it look the same" ("dark wood and red") –
and the reinstatement of its Continental menu classics,
with a few of returning chef Hidemasa Yamomoto's
"innovations creeping in", has this classic "back to its old
excellent form"; and it's still the place "to see the who's
who in Washington."

J. Paul's ◑ S   17 | 16 | 17 | $20
3218 M St., NW (bet. Potomac St. & Wisconsin Ave.),
202-333-3450
☑ This watering hole and weekend pit stop is "an easy
place to go" in Georgetown, with prime people-watching
from open window tables, an active thirtysomething nightlife,
raw bar and decent burgers, basics and brunch; yet,
withal a bit "plastic."

Kabul Caravan S   ▽ 22 | 19 | 20 | $23
Colonial Shopping Ctr., 1725 Wilson Blvd., Arlington, VA,
703-522-8394
■ The "shabby" locale of this award-winning Afghan
couldn't be more "misleading"; inside, an air of intrigue
and many "unusual", well-prepared Afghan specialties
make it perfect for "out-of-town guests"; an affordable
"set" tasting menu lets you try everything.

Kawasaki   ▽ 23 | 17 | 17 | $34
1140 19th St. NW (bet. M & L Sts.), 202-466-3798
☑ Top-flight sushi, a smart-looking setting and an accessible
address (below Dupont Circle) earn this Japanese a steady
international following; but from the standpoint of our
local surveyors, its staff could use diplomatic training and
its prices need devaluation.

Kazan   22 | 18 | 22 | $26
*McLean Shopping Ctr., 6813 Redmond Dr., McLean, VA,
703-734-1960*
☑ Always "gracious and welcoming", this Turkish old-timer
is a bit of "Istanbul in a Northern Virginia" storefront;
though it has "excellent lamb dishes", good wines and
many "little extras", the effect is marred by inconsistency
and a too "dark" setting: "cozy, but no cigar."

KINKEAD'S 🅂   25 | 22 | 22 | $37
*Red Lion Row, 2000 Pennsylvania Ave., NW (I St., bet. 20th
& 21st Sts.), 202-296-7700*
Bob Kinkead's "informal" modern American bistro opened
(near GWU) shortly pre-*Survey*, yet it zoomed to our Top
10 for Food, and, like his old 21 Federal, became an instant
power center; one goes downstairs for American tapas
and all-day snacking at a massive bar, upstairs for the
"innovative" seafood and meats; prime-time service and
open-kitchen decor leave room for improvement.

Kramerbooks &   16 | 15 | 14 | $17
Afterwords Cafe ◗🅂
*1517-21 Connecticut Ave., NW (bet. Q St., NW & Dupont
Circle), 202-387-1462*
4201 Wilson Blvd. (N. Stuart St.), Arlington, VA, 703-524-3900
☑ This Dupont Circle cafe/bookstore/performance space
has been a fixture since the '60s and, as always, sparks
the imagination: it's a "cool place to chill", "read a little,
eat a little and admire nose rings" over "light fare and
heavy conversation"; there's no "better at 2 AM"; its
expansion to Ballston is as welcome as "any port in a storm."

La Bergerie   24 | 23 | 23 | $40
*218 N. Lee St. (bet. King & Queen Sts.), Alexandria, VA,
703-683-1007*
■ A "romantic" townhouse in Old Town serving "old-style
French" food so "good" you can see why it's lasted; the
ambiance (like many of its customers) is from "an older
era" of "leisurely dining" and formality – this is one
restaurant where "guests are treated as guests"; also
noted for game and soufflés.

La Bonne Auberge S   23 | 22 | 22 | $33
Great Falls Shopping Ctr., 9835 Georgetown Pike (Walker Rd.), Great Falls, VA, 703-759-3877
☑ With French food and decor "on classical lines", this Virginia Valentine provides a change of pace from the nearby L'Auberge Chez François; its ambiance is "wonderful for special occasions", though performance-wise, it has "ups and downs."

La Brasserie S   22 | 20 | 21 | $31
239 Massachusetts Ave., NE (bet. 2nd & 3rd Sts.), 202-546-9154
☑ Its built-in advantage as the "only real restaurant on the Senate side" lets this "classic French bistro" charge "hefty prices" for "erratic food and service"; however, when it's good, there's no better place to welcome spring than its sidewalk terrace, or to cozy-up on "Christmas Eve."

La Chaumiere   22 | 21 | 21 | $30
2813 M St., NW (bet. 28th & 29th Sts.), 202-338-1784
☑ Save this Georgetown "farmhouse" for a cold winter night when you crave French comfort food and a hearthside seat; at its best, it's a "reminder" of how satisfying French cooking was pre-cholesterol and calorie consciousness, but reports that it "stopped using cheese sauce on the crêpe au crab" are unsettling.

La Colline   23 | 20 | 22 | $32
400 N. Capitol St., NW (bet. D & E Sts.), 202-737-0400
■ One books this Capitol Hill French bistro for its "adult service", "great food" and "a chance to harass legislators", not for its "boring decor"; a $17.50 prix fixe dinner "priced as a tax write-off" is further inducement.

La Cote d'Or Cafe S   24 | 22 | 22 | $33
6876 Lee Hwy. (bet. Washington Blvd. & Westmoreland St.), Arlington, VA, 703-538-3033
■ At this "friendly", "neighborhood bistro" in a suburban "low-rent district", Raymond Campet's steak frites and bouillabaisse cost nearly as much as they did at his ex La Brasserie on the Hill, but still bring "joy" to Falls Church.

LAFAYETTE S   24 | 25 | 23 | $41
Hay-Adams Hotel, 800 16th St., NW (H St.), 202-638-6600
■ With the arrival of celebrated New American chef Patrick Clark, power dining in this legendary room across from the White House is nearly as notable for the eating as for the viewing, "refined" atmosphere and "impeccable" service; rumor has it that the Commander in Chief tried to steal the chef, but got shot down by a bipartisan majority in Congress.

La Ferme [S] 22 | 23 | 21 | $34

7101 Brookville Rd. (bet. East-West Hwy. & Western Ave.), Chevy Chase, MD, 301-986-5255

◪ A "lovely setting" and "somewhat old-fashioned French food" are the main attractions at this Chevy Chase Country French; its clientele reports that it's "not a place that takes chances" and "you'll never love it, but always come back."

La Fourchette [S] 21 | 19 | 20 | $27

2429 18th St., NW (bet. Kalorama St. & Columbia Rd.), 202-332-3077

◪ Filled with "Francophiles" soaking up "Greenwich Village atmosphere" at the best sidewalk seats in Adams Morgan, there's "something about this place" that makes its "average French food seem very good", "average" prices a bargain, and its "luck-of-the-draw" service charming.

la Madeleine French Bakery & Cafe [S] 🚭 – | – | – | M

Mid-Pike Plaza, 11858 Rockville Pike (Montrose Rd.), Rockville, MD, 301-984-2270

7607 Old Georgetown Rd. (Commerce St.), Bethesda, MD, 301-215-9142

500 King St., Alexandria, VA, 703-739-2853

Forged-in-Texas chain of cafe/bakeries with wholesome, Continental-style breads and pastries, salads, sandwiches and light entrees, cafeteria-style service and faux French country house atmosphere; it's being welcomed to chic suburbs all around town: "great French breakfast with baguettes still warm"; "it works, very tasty."

La Miche [S] 22 | 21 | 21 | $34

7905 Norfolk Ave. (bet. Wisconsin Ave. & Old Georgetown Rd.), Bethesda, MD, 301-986-0707

■ Everything a suburban French is expected to be – from its ability to handle groups to the "sugar-free soufflé", this "heart of Bethesda" standby has earned its "solid" reputation serving "very good" seafood dishes at Downtown prices and, understandably, sees no reason to change.

La Mirabelle ▽ 21 | 20 | 21 | $29

6645 Old Dominion Dr. (McLean Sq.), McLean, VA, 703-893-8484

■ French storefront that's something of a private club where friends get together over "good buy" dinners ($13.95) or a "quiet" lunch; the "classic, heavy" food, though "good", is almost beside the point, it's the fellowship and "friendliest maitre d'" that pull this place together.

Landini Brothers S

<u>21</u> <u>19</u> <u>20</u> <u>$26</u>

115 King St. (Union St.), Alexandria, VA, 703-836-8404

☑ With a prime Old Town location and "good people working there", this Italian "tradition" is like a second "home" to local pols and businesspeople who appreciate its old-fashioned menu and off-menu seafood specials as a change from "trendy" pastarias; others don't.

La Tomate S

<u>−</u> <u>−</u> <u>−</u> <u>M</u>

1701 Connecticut Ave., NW (Dupont Circle), 202-667-5505

Germinating near Dupont Circle, with "great people-watching from the patio and window" seats, regulars go to "dine with friends" in an "utterly relaxed" environment; those who resent paying "a hefty price for lightweight" Italian food, "snotty" help and "densely packed small tables" say it's "not quite ripe."

L'AUBERGE CHEZ FRANCOIS S

<u>27</u> <u>26</u> <u>26</u> <u>$43</u>

332 Springvale Rd. (2 miles north of Georgetown Pike), Great Falls, VA, 703-759-3800

■ "Recommended" for everyone, this country French "inn" and "romantic" garden is the "perfect celebratory place" where "enchanted evenings" are a specialty along with hearty Alsatian cuisine; nearly 700 reviewers sigh "simply the best, year after year", "utterly reliable without being dull" and "a bargain for what you get"; so what if there's a "reservation hassle", "just go."

L'Auberge Provencale S

<u>−</u> <u>−</u> <u>−</u> <u>E</u>

L'Auberge Provencale , Rte. 340 (Rte. 50), White Post, VA, 703-837-1375, 800-638-1702

"An evening in France", "classics with an up-to-the-minute finish" "an out-of-city experience" — our surveyors wrote in to query "how could (we) overlook" this charming country inn, near Middleburg, run by a delightful French couple.

Lauriol Plaza S

<u>20</u> <u>17</u> <u>18</u> <u>$22</u>

1801 18th St., NW (S St.), 202-387-0035

☑ "Popular with East Duponters" for "streetside dining on a sunny corner", bold margaritas and a "nice mixture" of Mexican and Spanish dishes at a "wide price range"; complaints focus on housekeeping and eating inside where it's "not too comfortable."

Lavandou S

<u>23</u> <u>17</u> <u>20</u> <u>$30</u>

3321 Connecticut Ave., NW (bet. Macomb & Newark Sts.), 202-966-3002

■ "Paris has 100 places" like this "tiny", "affordable" Cleveland Park French bistro, but in DC it's such a "treasure" that you need a "shoehorn to get in"; however, it's "always a good fit", with "honest" Mediterranean cooking and a "cheerful" staff.

Lebanese Taverna S
23 | 19 | 20 | $22 |

*5900 Washington Blvd. (McKinley Rd.), Arlington, VA,
703-241-8681*
*2641 Connecticut Ave. (bet. Calvert St. & Woodley Rd.),
202-265-8681*

Lebanese Taverna Market
*4400 Old Dominion Dr. (Lee Hwy. & Lorcom Ln.), Arlington,
VA, 703-276-8681*
■ Boosting "foreign relations" with every bite of their
"delicious" Middle Eastern food and with "friendly"
smiles, these siblings "deliver on culinary promises in
somewhat cramped" and "vastly different" quarters in
Arlington ("homely") and Adams Morgan (happening).

Le Bon Cafe S ⌽
21 | 16 | 13 | $10 |

*210 2nd St., SE (bet. Pennsylvania Ave. & C St., SE),
202-547-7200*
1310 Braddock Pl. (West St.), Alexandria, VA, 703-519-1777
■ "Invaluable" for anyone who works, visits or lives on
Capitol Hill, this bite-sized cafe branched out to Alexandria
last summer (not rated) where its "creative menu" of salads
and "imaginative" sandwiches is amplified by pizzas, pastas,
grills and bistro classics; surveyors hope that staff "training"
was amplified as well.

Le Caprice S
24 | 20 | 22 | $37 |

2348 Wisconsin Ave., NW (Calvert St.), 202-337-3394
■ This "intimate" French keeps a "low profile" (like many
of its guests) in an Upper Georgetown row house, whose
cozy, "close quarters" oddly suit its "distinctive", "Alsatian-
light" cuisine; on Monday nights, its co-owners share
their passion for couscous à la Parisienne with a sell-out
$13.50-$20 prix fixe; a few find the help a bit "cold."

Ledo Pizza S ⌽
16 | 7 | 14 | $12 |

*7213 Muncaster Mill Rd. (bet. Redland & Shady Grove
Rds.), Gaithersburg, MD, 301-869-7900*
*Boulevard Shops, 14609 Baltimore Ave. (Rte. 1), Laurel,
MD, 301-498-5336*
*1319-H Rockville Pike (Twinbrook Pkwy.), Rockville, MD,
301-309-8484*
*5245 Kenwood Station (River Rd.), Bethesda, MD,
301-656-5336*
*Fairfax Circle Plaza, 9542-B Arlington Blvd. (bet. Rtes. 50 &
29/Fairfax Cir.), Fairfax, VA, 703-359-2818*
*Battlefield Shopping Ctr., 1037 Edwards Ferry Rd. (15
Bypass), Leesburg, VA, 703-777-9500*
See Baltimore Alphabetical Directory.

Le Gaulois 23 | 20 | 20 | $28
1106 King St. (bet. Fayette & Henry Sts.), Alexandria, VA, 703-739-9494
■ This "sentimental favorite" has been "so good for so long" that one could easily take the excellence of its "moderately" priced, bourgeois French cooking for granted – yet, at the same time, every service slip or "bit of dowdiness" at its brick-walled, Old Town location prompts nostalgia for the long defunct "old place in DC."

LE LION D'OR 26 | 24 | 25 | $54
1150 Connecticut Ave., NW (bet. 18th & M Sts.), 202-296-7972
■ Jean-Pierre Goyenvalle's Downtown classic (No. 4 for food in this *Survey*) is a perennial "reminder of why we love French cuisine"; he "approaches perfection" in signature dishes like Dover sole and soufflés and "impresses" dignitaries with the "impeccable" service in his "formal" dining room; if there's a downside here, it's the perception of being a bit "stuffy."

Le Mistral 22 | 20 | 21 | $29
223 Pennsylvania Ave., SE (3rd St.), 202-543-7747
■ Packed with a "who's who on Capitol Hill at lunch", this "reliable" row house bistro has "cornered" the "French cuisine market on the House side", with lobbyists competing for "fireside" seats in the airy front room; with so "few decent places" in the area, most Hilltoppers are happy to be seated anywhere and we hear few complaints.

Le Refuge 24 | 20 | 22 | $29
127 N. Washington St. (bet. King & Cameron Sts.), Alexandria, VA, 703-548-4661
◪ Remarkably good bouillabaisse, cassoulet and saucy plats du jour are served amidst "Left Bank" kitsch in this "tiny", "smoky" one-room Old Town "favorite" French; it can be a "disaster on a busy night", "intimate" and "romantic" when slow, and "reminds one of being in France."

Le Rivage [S] 21 | 21 | 20 | $30
1000 Water St., SW (bet. Maine Ave. & 9th St.), 202-488-8111
■ On the waterfront, yet untouristy in its approach to fresh seafood à la français, "efficient" about pre-theater service, and Gallic in its "good value": the sunny views speak for themselves at this "very dependable, solid French."

Les Halles ◐ [S] – | – | – | M
1201 Pennsylvania Ave., NW (12th St.), 202-347-6848
A handsome brass-and-wood French brasserie with "well-spaced tables" to accommodate its Pennsylvania Avenue "power" crowd and "really good" French-cut meat at "fair prices"; it's just the place to beef up your vocabulary with words like "*entrecôte*", "*bavette*" and "*steak frites*."

Le Vieux Logis
23 | 20 | 22 | $35

7925 Old Georgetown Rd. (Auburn Ave.), Bethesda, MD, 301-652-6816

◪ Scandinavian chefs add new interest to what's often considered just "another convenient country French place" in Bethesda; feeling "like a small French cottage", it's a "wonderful spot for lunch" if you can "block out two hours" to enjoy it; at other times: "too many tables, too noisy, too busy, too much."

Listrani's S
17 | 14 | 16 | $19

5100 MacArthur Blvd., NW (Dana Pl.), 202-363-0619

◪ Perennially popular pizza mover and Potomac local family "hangout" serving "simple stuff at a fair price" (i.e. salads, pastas and "healthy" plates); while food ratings range from "fantastico" to near zero, many a surveyor has its delivery number "programmed into the phone."

Lite 'n' Fair
∇ 22 | 7 | 17 | $14

Belle View Shopping Ctr., 1510 Belle View Blvd. (Fort Hunt Rd.), Alexandria, VA, 703-660-6085 S
1018 King St. (bet. Patrick & Henry Sts.), Alexandria, VA, 703-549-3711

◧ "Five-star food in a take-out box (and under $10") is the appeal of this "offbeat deli" in Old Town where a former Watergate chef and his family turn out Asian-influenced French and Italian dishes; there's no decor and little space, but its Belle View branch is a 'real' restaurant.

Little Fountain Cafe, The S
∇ 21 | 20 | 22 | $22

2339 18th St., NW (bet. Kalorama & Columbia Rds.), 202-462-8100

◪ Finding "a quiet place where people care" is especially delightful on the hottest block in Adams Morgan; this "very Euro", "organic" cafe is "undiscovered", has a "creative" chef and is still "a great bargain."

Little Viet Garden S
21 | 17 | 17 | $17

3012 Wilson Blvd. (Garfield Rd.), Arlington, VA, 703-522-9686

◪ A lively Clarendon Vietnamese with "alfresco" dining, live music and parking; yet it draws a very mixed response: "cooperative staff" vs. "waiter forgot us", "nice ambiance" vs. "tacky", "inventive" vs. "tastes like Cracker Jacks."

Louisiana Express Company S
20 | 8 | 14 | $14

4921 Bethesda Ave. (Arlington Rd.), Bethesda, MD, 301-652-6945

◧ Except for a few picky Louisianans, most "love" the "French Quarter cooking" at this "authentically dingy" New Orleans–style cafe, and the "characters" who dish it out; it's "fast", "fatty" and "cheap", and "the rotisserie Cajun chicken is hard to beat."

Luigino [S] 22 | 21 | 19 | $30

1100 New York Ave., NW (bet. H & 12th Sts.), 202-371-0595

■ "Building a following" in "Convention Center territory", this "classy Italian bistro" does a good job with pasta and "well-conceived", amply portioned trattoria dishes; an eating bar facing the open kitchen is "good for solo diners", and a way to sidestep lunchtime waits and "erratic" service.

Lulu's New Orleans Cafe [S] 12 | 16 | 14 | $18

1217 22nd St., NW (M St.), 202-861-5858

◪ An ersatz *Big Easy* "atmosphere may be everything" this West End happy hour "pick-up hell" has to offer, though a few insist Crescent City chefs could "learn Louisiana cooking" here; for most, it's "bad booze, bad food, bad service" – but it has a lulu of a jazz brunch.

Madeo [S] 20 | 21 | 20 | $28

1113 23rd St., NW (bet. L & M Sts.), 202-457-0057

◪ The airy garden room at this West End Cal-Italian is such a come-on that its "pleasant" food (with "offbeat" combinations) and "spotty" service don't always meet "expectations"; still, it's a popular pre–Kennedy Center pit stop, also good for a "sunny brunch."

Maison Blanche 23 | 23 | 22 | $40

1725 F St., NW (bet. 17th & 18th Sts.), 202-842-0070

■ In case you "haven't been since '92", this "plush" place near the White House is a "trifle stuffy" (and "too '80s"), but is awfully "elegant" with "first-rate" Contemporary French food and an impressive pre-theater prix fixe; it's easy to "forget how good it is."

Marquis de Rochambeau ◐ [S] ▽ 10 | 20 | 12 | $27

3108 M St., NW (bet. 31st St. & Wisconsin Ave.), 202-333-0393/4

■ A "Fellini-esque experience", a "serious hoot", this "wild" Georgetown French supper club and cabaret has a "campy" bordello setting with a "late-night crowd of French ex-pats and lounge lizards"; it has to be seen to be believed, but "don't eat" there – it's way too expensive.

Martin's Tavern [S] 16 | 17 | 16 | $21

1264 Wisconsin Ave., NW (N St.), 202-333-7370

■ This simple wooden tavern is one of the few places "left in Georgetown that's real" offering "old-fashioned" American "barroom dining" and "solid" value in a "restful", unchanging setting; go for "Sunday breakfast with *The Post*" or a "romantic" late supper.

Matuba 🅂　　　　22 | 14 | 20 | $20
2915 Columbia Pike (Walter Reed St.), Arlington, VA,
703-521-2811
4918 Cordell Ave. (Old Georgetown Rd.), Bethesda, MD,
301-652-7449
■ "Unpretentious" suburban Japanese duo that may be
"downscale" with respect to prices and settings, but are
upscale in the "quality and preparation" of their sushi and
cooked dishes and in their "cheerful" help.

Melrose 🅂　　　　24 | 24 | 23 | $38
Park Hyatt Hotel, 24th & M Sts., NW, 202-955-3899
■ It "never feels like a hotel", yet this "tranquil" West
Ender offers round-the-clock amenities including the
"best" afternoon tea "outside London's Dorchester Hotel"
and boasts a versatile Contemporary American kitchen
("inventive but not ridiculous") and "professional" staff;
its "bargain" prix fixe dinner is an ideal introduction.

Meskerem ◕🅂　　　　21 | 20 | 19 | $19
2434 18th St., NW (Columbia Rd.), 202-462-4100
■ While dining à la Ethiope, scooping up incendiary
stews with spongy bread, isn't everyone's idea of "fun",
aficionados favor this 18th Street standby for its "attractive
setting" and the "nuance and variety" of the food; if you
haven't tried it, "sharing a meal" with friends here can be
an exotic experience.

Metro Center Grille 🅂　　　　20 | 20 | 21 | $24
Marriott at Metro Ctr., 775 12th St., NW (H St.), 202-737-2200
◪ The departure of chef Melissa Berringer puts the above
food rating and the direction of this "barnlike" Convention
Center hotel dining room in doubt since, apart from its
location, the interesting food was the major draw; an
all-you-can-eat downstairs American buffet is popular for
stuffing "stuffed shirts."

Mick's 🅂　　　　16 | 17 | 17 | $17
2401 Pennsylvania Ave., NW (24th St.), 202-331-9613
1220 19th St., NW (bet. M & N Sts.), 202-785-2866
Fair Oaks Mall (Junction Rtes. 50 & 66), Fairfax, VA,
703-934-9716
Springfield Mall (Franconia Rd.), Springfield, VA,
703-971-6106
◪ "Red, white and blue" and utterly "average", these
postgraduate, family saloons major in "kid-friendliness" and
happy hour, with a minor in "frat-boy food at adult prices";
they get their best grades for "fried green tomatoes", salads
and "stupendous desserts."

Mike's American Grill S 19 | 18 | 18 | $18 |
6210 Backlick Rd. (Old Keene Mill Rd.), Springfield, VA,
703-644-7100
■ They "aimed at ordinary and scored a bullseye" with
this "good ole American" in Springfield; its "no-fuss bar",
burgers, salads, and prime rib menu and "dark", business-
class space draw the kind of crowds the devil invented
beepers for; with "not many places in (the area) to get a
nice meal, here's one."

Miss Saigon S ▽ 21 | 16 | 19 | $18 |
1847 Columbia Rd., NW (18th St.), 202-667-1900
◪ Playing off the B'way hit, this Adams Morgan Vietnamese
newcomer has a stagy set (slick black and twinkly lights)
and some "solid" menu performers (especially the clay
pot dishes and grills), but gets mixed reviews.

Mixtec S 19 | 10 | 14 | $15 |
1792 Columbia Rd., NW (18th St.), 202-332-1011
◪ Put this tiny Columbia Road taqueria on your gastronomic
map for its "authentic" tacos al carbon (fajitas without
the frills), tamales and meal-in-a-sandwich tortas; it's
"authentically third world" in atmosphere which some
like and some don't.

Monocle, The 17 | 16 | 18 | $26 |
107 D St., NE (1st St.), 202-546-4488
■ This popular Capitol Hill "institution" functions as an
extension of the Senate cloakroom – meaning that
"efficient service (for pols) and an old-boy atmosphere
are the norm"; the food is average American.

Montego Cafe ◐ S 18 | 15 | 17 | $18 |
2437 18th St., NW (bet. Belmont & Columbia Rds.),
202-745-1002
■ A "boisterous Jamaican" in Adams Morgan, with
cheap, earthy food, a sidewalk terrace ("ignore inside")
and a "slow pace"; in the DC heat, with reggae playing
and a Red Stripe, "sit outside", "mellow down easy" and
"pretend" to be in Kingston.

Montgomery's Grille S 16 | 18 | 17 | $19 |
7200 Wisconsin Ave. (Bethesda Ave.), Bethesda, MD,
301-654-3595
◪ "Excitingly noisy", if you're part of the "Georgetown-
meets-Bethesda" singles scene, this vast, all-purpose
beer-'n'-burger American bistro is also where Bethesda
professionals "do lunch" and take their families for brunch;
most find "nothing special" about the food or service.

MORRISON-CLARK INN [S] 25 | 25 | 23 | $37
Morrison-Clark Inn, 1015 L St., NW (bet. 11th St. & Massachusetts Ave.), 202-898-1200
■ Everything comes together at this beautifully restored Downtown Victorian, making it "one of the top" restaurants in the city; Susan Lindeborg's food is "wonderfully" American "with a light touch" and some "Southern" accents, her desserts are "Betty Crocker gone to heaven" and the pervading spirit is "gracious" and "genteel"; the only downer is the neighborhood.

MORTON'S OF CHICAGO [S] 25 | 21 | 23 | $45
3251 Prospect St., NW (Wisconsin Ave.), 202-342-6258
8075 Leesburg Pike (Gallows Rd.), Tysons Corner, VA, 703-883-0800
◪ "You want beef? go here; you want intimacy? go elsewhere"; this A-1 "men's-den" chain from the Windy City serves the "best and biggest steaks in town" (plus lobster and soufflés) to well-hooved carnivores who'd "eat there every night if their doctors would let them."

Mr. K's [S] 24 | 24 | 23 | $38
2121 K St., NW (bet 21st & 22nd Sts.), 202-331-8868
◪ A "serene" showcase for Chinese "haute" cuisine as served in Hong Kong, where you "step through the door and become royalty"; this K Street luxury lion "always impresses", however, some prefer less: "too highbrow", "only the Japanese can afford."

Mrs. Simpson's [S] 22 | 22 | 22 | $32
2915 Connecticut Ave., NW (Cathedral Ave.), 202-332-8300
◪ Its unlimited champagne brunch ($15.95) is a fitting tribute to the Windsor/Simpson romance, the theme that gives special "charm" to this boite and its light, lower-priced, contemporary fare, but which isn't always reflected by the help ("make you feel like a stranger").

Mr. Yung's [S] 20 | 10 | 17 | $17
740 6th St., NW (bet. G & H Sts.), 202-628-1098
■ A Downtown "dim sum favorite", this simple Cantonese storefront is one of the few places in Chinatown with "atmosphere" ("intimate" with a good buzz) and a really "helpful" staff; frequent lunchers tout its "traditional dishes", but a few disparage it as "yesterday."

Music City Roadhouse – | – | – | I
1050 30th St., NW (bet. M & K Sts.), 202-337-4444
"Plain, good old country cooking" at down-home prices is the deal at this Southern roadhouse replica in Georgetown, and it's a good one – $12.95 for all you can eat, "family-style", with kids under six eating free (half-price under 12) and there's live country music and a rollicking gospel brunch.

Mykonos
    -   -   -   M

1835 K St., NW (19th St.), 202-331-0370

Moving to a "larger, nicer locale", on K Street's "lawyers' alley", put this "generous" Greek in a strategic spot; "if you like Greek food", chances are you'll enjoy M's "tasty" menu and "warm atmosphere", not to mention the modest bill.

Nam's
    ▽ 23   9   20 $14

11220 Georgia Ave. (University Blvd.), Wheaton, MD, 301-933-2525

Nam's of Bethesda
4928 Cordell Ave. (bet. Woodmont Ave. & Old Georgetown Rd.), Bethesda, MD, 301-652-2635

■ In Wheaton, a "hole-in-the-wall" with great Vietnamese food – "crowded, noisy but so Saigonese" and cheap; its Bethesda offshoot (unrated) serves the same "delicious, complex" dishes, just as "professionally", in an attractive, wood-trimmed room; both are even cheaper at lunch.

Nam Viet S
    21   13   18 $16

1127 N. Hudson St. (Wilson Blvd.), Arlington, VA, 703-522-7110

■ "Best on block" Vietnamese, and, given Clarendon's "competitive market", that "proves" a lot about its "good, consistent food", "clean", "pleasant setting" and "quick" service; regulars like the pho, garden rolls and grilled pork.

Nathans Restaurant S
    18   17   18 $29

3150 M St., NW (Wisconsin Ave.), 202-338-2000

◪ An old-fashioned corner tavern favored by what's left of "Georgetown's chic" for barroom wining and back-room "sophisticated" dining on "wonderful" pasta and veal; after 11 PM, "a collegiate crowd descends"; as you'd expect, the help acts more "serious about serving" the diners than the daters.

New Heights S
    24   23   22 $35

2317 Calvert St., NW (Connecticut Ave.), 202-234-4110

◪ "Daring", decorative and "different", this new age American goes for "bizarre combos" – "wonderful, when they work", but at times the menu's "so creative" there's "nothing to eat"; an art-filled setting, overlooking Rock Creek Park, and "stylish" staff add to the "stimulating" ambiance.

NICHOLAS S
    26   25   25 $45

Mayflower Hotel, 1127 Connecticut Ave., NW (bet. L & DeSalles Sts.), 202-347-8900

■ Tino Buggio, the "Cadillac chef" at this "old-school" Downtowner, and his "excellent" Contemporary food (now refocused on seafood), get "better every year", as shown by ratings which climbed to the top five for food and service; though largely "unheralded" by the media, it's "surprising who you see here", i.e. "definitely power" at lunch.

Nizam's Restaurant S　　22　18　20　$26
Village Green Shopping Ctr., 523 Maple Ave. W. (Rte. 123), Vienna, VA, 703-938-8948
☑ Known for its "addictive" doner kebab, this "intimate" Vienna storefront is a mecca for the local Turkish community, though exactly "how close" the mezes and its "fine lamb" and eggplant dishes "come" to Istanbul is debatable; most agree your odds are "better when Nizam is there."

NORA　　25　23　23　$40
2132 Florida Ave., NW (bet. Connecticut & Mass. Aves.), 202-462-5143
■ Nora practically invented "food that cares", and in her romantically "rustic" townhouse she provides the "latest" in "fresh, delicious" and "organically correct" American dining; despite reservations about pacing and pricing, hundreds of surveyors laud her "nearly perfect restaurant" – though "since Bill and Hill glommed onto this gem", it's "hard for former regulars" to get near the place.

Notte Luna S　　20　20　19　$26
809 15th St., NW (bet. H & I Sts.), 202-408-9500
☑ A "pulsing", neon-lit, Cal-Italiano convenient for a "quicky" Downtown lunch or "after-work" drink, for "a jump into" the club scene or having "White House staffers at the next table"; many find its pizza and pasta less interesting than the "wild music", sidewalk patio and "bathroom Berlitz."

OBELISK　　25　22　23　$45
2029 P St., NW (bet. 20th & 21st Sts.), 202-872-1180
■ A meal at DC's No. 2 Italian is "like dining in its owner [Peter Pastan's] home" on "lovely" but "limited" prix fixe menus, inspired by Northern Italy, served by "gracious" people in an "understated" room; Pastan is a "purist in the best sense", evidenced by his "incredible pastries, pastas, soups" and breads.

O'Brien's Pit Barbecue S　　16　10　11　$15
387 E. Gude Dr. (Crabbs Branch Way), Rockville, MD, 301-340-8596
☑ Still "good enough for government work", but what was once Rockville's sole source for "decent BBQ", a cafeteria-style canteen, is less "appealing" now that there's "new competition" like Red, Hot & Blue.

Occidental Grill S　　22　23　22　$32
Willard Complex (Pennsylvania Ave. & 14th St.), 202-783-1475
☑ A "classy joint" that's "easy to dine" at, combining "Washington tradition" with "good American food" and "lots of attention"; though it's pricey and "variable" when busy, it's "an important restaurant that makes you feel that way" while conveying a "sense of place and history."

Odeon Cafe 🅂
17 | 17 | 16 | $22

1714 Connecticut Ave., NW (bet. R & S Sts.), 202-328-6228

◼ One of the first of the "big bowl" pasta "purveyors" draws Dupont Circle crowds into a "hot, dark", loud space for what is variously described as "delectable" or "dull" food.

O'Donnell's Restaurant 🅂
17 | 15 | 18 | $22

8301 Wisconsin Ave. (Battery Lane), Bethesda, MD, 301-656-6200

◼ For all the bashing of this "upscale Ho-Jo" fish house and its "geriatric" appeal, it does have "fresh" if "rather plain" fish and treats its elders "with tenderness"; "it's hard to dupicate the old days", but the rum buns and dishes "dripping with butter" aren't a bad try.

Old Angler's Inn 🅂
22 | 25 | 21 | $40

10801 MacArthur Blvd. (1 mile past intersection with Clara Barton Pkwy.), Potomac, MD, 301-365-2425

◼ "Few spots are more romantic" than the sun-splashed terrace of this rustic "refuge" or its fireside and now, it's "back up there again", serving some of the area's most innovative Contemporary American food; service lags a bit behind, as does the ambiance indoors.

Old Ebbitt Grill ◖🅂
19 | 21 | 19 | $25

675 15th St., NW (bet. F & G Sts.), 202-347-4801

◼ "In the heart of it all", this "bustling", "polished-brass" and burnished-wood American is a "gathering spot" for politicos as well as tourists and usually manages "to please everyone" from those in "jeans" to "starched collars"; it's hard to "argue with success", but dissenters fault unevenness and waits.

Old Glory All American Barbecue ◖🅂
18 | 18 | 18 | $18

3139 M St., NW (bet. Wisconsin Ave. & 31st St.), 202-337-3406

◼ A "gimmicky" Georgetown rib joint that gives sporty "collegians" a "change from bar food" and a chance to cool off after the game; its BBQ and sides get added "zing" from buckets of beer and hot sauces, "Elvis and Patsy Cline", a "high-energy staff" and more activity than anyone "over 25" can handle.

Otello
– | – | – | M

1329 Connecticut Ave. NW (½ block south of Dupont Metro Station), 202-429-0209

One of those family-run, "red-checker-tablecloth" places that give "neighborhood" Italians a good name; near Dupont Circle and reputedly a "Clinton crowd" pleaser, we're told it has the "best calamari alla Luciana in the USA", good pastas and moderate prices.

Outback Steakhouse S   20 | 17 | 19 | $20
7720 Woodmont Ave. (bet. Old Georgetown Rd. &
Wisconsin Ave.), Bethesda, MD, 301-913-0176
12609 Wisteria Dr. (Great Seneca Hwy.), Germantown,
MD, 301-353-9499
150 Elden St. #100 (Herndon Pkwy.), Herndon, VA,
703-318-0999
Backlick Ctr., 6651 Backlick Rd. (Old Keene Mill Rd.),
Springfield, VA, 703-912-7531
14580 Potomac Mills Rd. (Bixby Rd.), Woodbridge, VA,
703-490-5336
The Colonnade, 5702 Union Mill Rd. (Rte. 29), Clifton, VA,
703-818-0804
Twinbrooke Shopping Ctr., 9579 Braddock Rd. (Twinbrooke
Dr.), Fairfax, VA, 703-978-6283
Arlington Forest Shopping Ctr., 4821 N. 1st St. (off Rte. 50
at Park Dr.), Arlington, VA, 703-527-0063
◪ An Aussie-accented "answer to the question 'where's
the beef'?" – this chain's response is "cheap steak" with
trimmings like "bloomin' onion", cheese fries and the
"coldest beer on the planet"; the "mob scene", "long
waits" and "tons of fun" come without charge.

Oval Room   – | – | – | E
800 Conn. Ave., NW (H St.), 202-463-8700
A modish, intimate Contemporary American near the White
House, opened at press time by the talents behind the suave
and creative Bombay Club and 701; if it runs true to form, it
could become the '90s version of Maison Blanche and
Sans Souci where friendly nods foreshadow major events.

Palais du Chocolat S   23 | 17 | 17 | $9
3309 Conn. Ave., NW (bet. Macomb & Ordway Sts.),
202-363-2462
◪ Chocolate and cappuccino rate a "big oui" at this
Cleveland Park pastry/coffee stop where a "limited" lunch
menu leaves room to splurge on "to-die-for" espresso
brownies and other desserts; "so-so" service and un-
palacelike storefront decor are no match for the sweets.

PALLADIN S   24 | 23 | 23 | $43
The Watergate Hotel, 2650 Virginia Ave., NW (New
Hampshire Ave.), 202-298-4455
◪ Jean-Louis Palladin's "river view" bistro offers his
celebrated "distinctive" Gascon cuisine "at a better
price"; what you get is "wonderful" food (if he's not "on a
holiday"), Kennedy Center convenience (which can "feel
rushed") and formal ("stuffy") surroundings and service;
in sum, "while it's no cheap eats, it's one of DC's best."

PALM, THE S　　　　23 | 19 | 21 | $38
1225 19th St., NW (bet. M & N Sts.), 202-293-9091
☑ A "bastion" of "bare-knuckles" dining with "great" beef,
lobster spinach and fries; post-rehab and sans sawdust,
it's still a "place where you aren't afraid to spill something",
and where it takes a big mouth to deal with the steaks
and the waiters.

Pan Asian Noodles & Grill　　19 | 13 | 17 | $15
2020 P St., NW (20th St.), 202-872-8889 S
1018 Vermont Ave., NW (bet. 14th & 15th Sts.), 202-783-8899
☑ Whether "broke and hungry" or merely "paying for
lunch", you can "slurp your way to happiness" at these
high-tech noodle shops for a pittance; Metro-convenient,
with a multi-Asian twist, they offer enough "variety" of
noodles, seafood soups and grills to "eat here once a week."

Panjshir S　　　　24 | 16 | 21 | $19
224 W. Maple Ave. (Rte. 123), Vienna, VA, 703-281-4183
■ Although this attractive, "hard-working" Afghan serves
"very good food at reasonable prices" (and get high food
ratings), it remains something of a "local secret"; enough
neighbors enjoy its "interesting" combination ingredients
and "subtle" spicing to produce frequent crowds and waits.

Paolo's S　　　　20 | 20 | 19 | $22
1303 Wisconsin Ave., NW (N St.), 202-333-7353 ◐
1801 Rockville Pike (Randolph Rd.), Rockville, MD,
301-984-2211
Reston Town Ctr., Market & Fountain Sts., Reston, VA,
703-318-8920
■ With some of the hottest locations and longest hours in
the area, many people eat at these Cal-Italian fern bars
"more than anywhere else"; though "trendy", they
"balance" food and fun with a pizza/pasta/salad menu that
encourages free-form eating and easy-going friendliness.

Parioli S　　　　21 | 19 | 18 | $26
4800 Elm St. (Wisconsin Ave.), Bethesda, MD, 301-951-8600
☑ This Bethesda Italian is packed nightly with "le tout
Potomac" who come for its "authentic" homemade fare and
generic pricing (i.e. all pastas $6 at lunch, $9 at night), but
who complain about the "din" and "cavalier" service.

Pasha Cafe S　　　▽ 22 | 14 | 22 | $16
Cherrydale Shopping Ctr., 2109 N. Pollard St. (Military Rd.),
Arlington, VA, 703-528-2126
■ Billed as a "Mediterranean" and tasting "mmm-mmm
good", this new Arlington cafe features the food of Egypt,
serving interesting versions of familiar Middle Eastern
appetizers and kebabs at "dirt cheap" prices; it's building
enough of a following for "slow" service to be a problem.

Pasta Place, The ● S ∇ 16 | 18 | 16 | $21

Washington Harbour, 3050 K St., NW (Wisconsin Ave.), 202-342-3535

☑ Spillover crowds for what some deem the "best food at (Washington) Harbour" don't say as much about the mid-priced pasta, pizza, piccatas and Caesar salad as it does about Potomac sunsets and people-watching from the piazza.

Pasta Plus S – | – | – | M

Center Plaza, 209 Gorman Ave. (bet. Rtes. 1 & 198E), Laurel, MD, 301-498-5100

"An excellent value" Italian in a "surprising location", where an "unusually savvy" team cooks "homemade" pasta, pizza and "superior" fish and meats like they do in Abruzzi; it's so popular that, if it's much after 6 PM, you can't get in.

Patisserie Cafe Didier S 24 | 16 | 17 | $16

3206 Grace St., NW (bet. M & K Sts.), 202-342-9083

■ Just off the canal in Georgetown is an "enchanting hideaway", where "scents of croissants and hyacinths" whet appetites for Didier Schoner's "incredible" pastries — the equal of any in Paris or Vienna; open for Continental breakfast through PM tea, it's "wonderful" for a light lunch.

PEKING GOURMET INN S 24 | 16 | 21 | $23

Culmore Shopping Ctr., 6029 Leesburg Pike, Falls Church, VA, 703-671-8088

☑ Most go to this celebrated Falls Church Chinese for pan-fried dumplings and the rewarding Peking duck, though lately, attention has focused on its "light sauces" and "unusual" custom-grown produce; critics would like to dispense with the waits and "escalating" prices.

Perry's ● S 20 | 22 | 17 | $23

1811 Columbia Rd., NW (18th St.), 202-234-6218

■ "Nothing can top" its Adams Morgan roofdeck for "sushi under the stars", or, when the "happening scene" at this next-wave fusion moves inside in winter, to "martinis on the couch", late-night music and the drag-show brunch; "ever-evolving", always an "eyeful", "loud" and "erratic", it's not the best food, "but the best place to eat it."

Persepolis S 18 | 14 | 17 | $20

7130 Wisconsin Ave. (bet. Bethesda & Miller Aves.), Bethesda, MD, 301-656-9339

☑ Perceptions of the Persian food at this "Bethesda bargain" shift from applause for "fresh, "well-seasoned" kebabs, "unfailingly good" eggplant and the "best fessenjan" (savory stew) to shrugs: "nothing special", "reliable but boring"; no one thinks the food is helped by the "cavernous", "dark green" setting or over-cool waiters.

PESCE S   23 │ 15 │ 20 │ $28
2016 P St., NW (bet. Dupont Circle & 20th St.),
202-466-FISH
■ "Practically perfect" – as you'd expect at top toques
Roberto Donna's and Jean-Louis Palladin's seafood bistro;
the fish is "sparkling" fresh, and served in a "simple-is-
perfect" Dupont Circle storefront; though its "moderate"
prices are "a bargain for the level of the food" (best
seafood in *Survey*) and "intelligent" service, some expect
to pay even less at what also functions as a fish market.

Phillips Flagship S   14 │ 14 │ 14 │ $22
900 Water St., SW (9th St.), 202-488-8495
Phillips Seafood Grill ◐ S
American Center/Signet Bank Bldg., 8330 Boone Blvd.
(bet. Rtes. 7 & 23), Tysons Corner, VA, 703-442-0400
◪ Waterfront locations spawn tourists, "confusion" and
waits at these commercialized "Maryland" fish houses
thus requiring "hometown people" to time visits and
choose dishes carefully; since surveyors still complain
about "flavorless" food, it makes one wonder how the
new Tysons Corner outlet will do without a view.

Pho 75 S ⊘   21 │ 5 │ 15 │ $10
1711 Wilson Blvd. (Quinn St.), Arlington, VA, 703-525-7355
1510 University Blvd. E. (bet. N. Glebe Rd. & Pershing Dr.),
Langley Park, MD, 301-434-7844
3103 Graham Rd. (Rte. 50), Falls Church, VA, 703-204-1490
■ These Vietnamese soup kitchens add a dimension to
"cheap eats" with meal-in-a-bowl, "cure-whatever-ails-
you" noodle soups and with "communal" seating that
fosters informal language lessons; regulars warn that the
"meats are fatty", there's "zero decor" and the pungent
"fish sauce" should not be mistaken for soy.

Pier 7 S   15 │ 16 │ 17 │ $24
Channel Inn, 650 Water St., SW (bet. 7th St. & Maine Ave.,
SW), 202-554-2500
◪ Local pols, pol-watchers and feds go to "smell the coffee"
and listen to jazz, leaving the "dull" food for tourists and
Arena Stage–goers; word that it has "improved" is welcome.

Pilin Thai S   ▽ 22 │ 20 │ 23 │ $17
116 W. Broad St. (Rte. 29), Falls Church, VA, 703-241-5850
■ "Top value" Thai in Falls Church that compares
favorably to other Thais with "excellent food", notably
fish and pad Thai, and "attentive service"; its "warm"
atmosphere, with "lots of chatter", is a good sign.

Pines of Italy [S] 17 | 10 | 16 | $15

237 N. Glebe Rd. (Pershing Dr.), Arlington, VA, 703-524-4969
556 S. 22nd St. (Army Navy Dr.), Crystal City, VA, 703-271-0511

◪ A "worn" Arlington "family food" Italian with a "check so low you'll think it's a mistake"; on the down slope, it seems to be "outshined" in the cheap eats department by new competition.

Pines of Rome [S] – | – | – | M

4709 Hampden Ln. (Wisconsin Ave.), Bethesda, MD, 301-657-8775

We got a lot of flack for leaving this "great value" Bethesda Southern Italian "standby" off this year's questionnaire, especially given the fact that it's been "packed with appreciative diners for over 20 years"; they go for white pizza and grilled fish, and its casual "chow-down style", but some call it a "used to be."

Pizzeria Paradiso [S] 24 | 18 | 18 | $18

2029 P St., NW (bet. 20th & 21st Sts.), 202-223-1245

■ "Defining pizza in DC" with a "smoky crisp crust" and "high-quality toppings, judiciously applied" – this Obelisk sibling pizzeria off Dupont Circle is the "best in the area, perhaps anywhere"; everything is served with "enthusiasm", including fresh salads and fine focaccia sandwiches; go early or late, since the waits are strictly "Pizzeria Purgatorio."

Planet Hollywood ◐ [S] 14 | 22 | 16 | $18

1101 Pennsylvania Ave. NW (11th St.), 202-783-7827

◪ A Hard Rock remake, with a Hollywood cast; tourists, teens and film buffs interested in movie memorabilia and film clips – it seems that covers almost everybody – line up for the experience; though not a "dining experience", its wide-ranging American-Eclectic menu, especially burgers and desserts, is low risk and affordable enough so you can make the near-obligatory purchase at the shop on the way out.

Pleasant Peasant [S] 21 | 21 | 20 | $28

Mazza Gallerie, 5300 Wisconsin Ave., NW (bet. Jennifer St. & Western Ave.), 202-364-2500

Peasant Restaurant & Bar, The [S]

Market Sq., 801 Pennsylvania Ave., NW, 202-638-2140

■ On Pennsylvania Avenue, it provides a "corporate setting for business meals", but also "works well" for socializing and "celebrity watching"; the Mazza Gallerie Peasant is best "known" for its "shopping break" desserts; the food at both is "nothing fancy", but as the name promises, "pleasant"; waiting and attitude can be unpleasant.

Polly's Cafe ● S   20 | 19 | 18 | $17
1342 U St., NW (bet. 13th & 14th Sts.), 202-265-8385
■ A "convivial" New U "trailblazer" that's "welcoming" in
winter by the fire, though its laid-back regulars provide
"local color" year-round; you "get lots for the money", but
going beyond burgers/brunch takes you into "rough" ground.

Potowmack Landing S   16 | 21 | 16 | $23
*Washington Sailing Marina, George Washington Pkwy.
(1½ miles south of National Airport), Alexandria, VA,
703-548-0001*
◪ "The view's" the draw at this rustic "hideaway" near
National Airport, but why the "normal" American food and
"indifferent" service aren't in sync with the "unbeatable"
waterside setting and plane/boat-watching is a puzzlement.

Powerscourt S   22 | 22 | 22 | $33
*Phoenix Park Hotel, 520 N. Capitol St., NW (Mass. Ave.),
202-737-3776*
■ "A best-kept secret" with a constant "power hum", this
"elegant" Union Station–area dining room reconciles
seeming contradictions; it's "friendly" yet "formal", mixing
"romance, politics and great food" and proving that "gourmet
Irish" is not an oxymoron; "intimacy makes it special."

PRIME RIB, THE   25 | 24 | 24 | $42
2020 K St., NW (bet. 20th & 21st Sts.), 202-466-8811
■ "Deliciously politically (and gastronomically) incorrect"
this icon serves the best prime rib, steak, salad and crab
imperial in town; its "dark, plush surroundings" are lined
with "DC brass", its "waiters are pros" and 'everybody',
socially speaking, comes to "watch the goings on"; even
its few critics say fondly: "frozen in 1947, but well prepared."

Primi Piatti   23 | 21 | 20 | $30
2013 I St., NW (bet. 20th & 21st Sts.), 202-223-3600 S
*8045 Leesburg Pike (Gallows Rd.), Tysons Corner, VA,
703-893-0300*
■ "Upscale" trattorias that are "sophisticated", "brassy",
"bustling"; their "tasty" antipasti, pasta and grills, "sidewalk
dining" (in DC) and "moderate prices" explain why they're
"crowded and noisy", with at times "inconsistent service."

Provence   – | – | – | E
2401 Pennsylvania Ave., NW (L St.), 202-296-1166
It didn't take long for bec fins to discover that Yannick Cam
(ex Yannick's and Le Pavillon) was cooking distinctive French
Provençal food in an elegant, relaxed, Mediterranean setting
in the West End; he revolutionized tapas at trendy Coco
Loco, and gives appetizers here a mouthwatering Gallic
spin, but save room for his equally enticing entrees.

Queen Bee S
22 | 12 | 18 | $17

3181 Wilson Blvd. (Washington Blvd.), Arlington, VA,
703-527-3444

■ "Good food, cheap prices, helpful staff — you can't lose
on a meal" at this Clarendon Vietnamese though the cost
includes "bearing lines", "close-packed" seating and
"hurry-you-out" teamwork; "great dishes" like "grilled
chicken in lemon grass" make it pay off.

Rabieng S
▽ 23 | 19 | 22 | $25

Glen Forest Shopping Ctr., 5892 Leesburg Pike (bet. Glen
Forest Dr. & Payne St.), Falls Church, VA, 703-671-4222

■ Living in the shadow of its nearby sibling, Duangrat,
(the *Survey's* top Thai), this simple storefront is often seen
from a relative perspective: "quiet version", "as good as,
just more informal"; though one "can order from Duangrat's
menu", Rabieng's unique country dishes from northeastern
Thailand set it apart; definitely "worth a try."

Red, Hot & Blue S
21 | 15 | 18 | $17

1600 Wilson Blvd. (Pierce St.), Arlington, VA, 703-276-7427
3014 Wilson Blvd. (N. Garfield St.), Arlington, VA, 703-243-1510
677 Main St. (Rte. 216), Laurel, MD, 301-953-1943
Canterbury Ctr., 8637 Sudley Rd. (bet. Rtes. 234 & 28),
Manassas, VA, 703-330-4847
1120 19th St., NW (bet. M & L Sts.), 202-466-6731
16811 Crabbs Branch Way (Shady Grove Rd.),
Gaithersburg, MD, 301-948-7333

■ These Memphis-style BBQ joints mostly live up to the
"hype": "not since Adam and Eve have ribs deserved so
much attention", "worth the hassle and crowd", "doesn't
get better"; they're endorsed by all political parties, who
"couldn't wait for the Downtown branch to open."

RED SAGE S
22 | 26 | 21 | $37

605 14th St., NW (F St.), 202-638-4444

☑ Nearly half our surveyors have gotten heated up at this
Southwestern-theme Downtowner, a "Roy and Dale on
LSD" extravaganza with an expanded upstairs chili
bar-cum-trattoria and a spectacular "dining theater"
downstairs; sure, it's "inconsistent", "arrogant" and
"loud" and there's "nothing (to eat) without heat", but it
gets very high ratings and lots of repeat traffic from
people who vote with their feet.

Red Sea ◑ S
18 | 11 | 15 | $18

2463 18th St., NW (bet. Kalorama Rd.), 202-483-5000

☑ Incendiary Ethiopian food is not for the squeamish, but
it's copious and cheap, thus this Adams Morgan standby's
post-Survey spruce-up, new vegetarian dishes and outdoor
cafe are most appreciated; the only "sore spot" is service.

Renato 🅂　　　21 | 19 | 19 | $27
10120 River Rd. (Potomac Pl.), Potomac, MD, 301-365-1900
■ A Potomac "neighborhood" trattoria that's "friendly",
"consistent", good with kids, and "willing to modify dishes";
in other words, it acts like it "wants your business", thus
customers cut it slack for its "homey" food and occasional
"uneven" service.

Restaurant, The 🅂　　　24 | 25 | 23 | $38
Ritz-Carlton at Tysons II, 1700 Tysons Blvd. (Galleria,
International Blvd.), McLean, VA, 703-506-4300 x7488
■ Despite an unimaginative name, this "plush" retreat easily
wins "best of show in Tysons"; relatively "undiscovered",
it offers a "lovely dining experience", with "excellent"
Continental food, "polished presentation" and "service
like the old days"; its "elegant" tea, lavish Sunday brunch
and the "super" Friday night seafood buffet are all a must.

RIO GRANDE CAFE 🅂　　　22 | 18 | 19 | $19
4919 Fairmont Ave. (Old Georgetown Rd.), Bethesda, MD,
301-656-2981
4301 N. Fairfax Dr. (Glebe Rd.), Arlington, VA, 703-528-3131
Reston Town Ctr., 1827 Library St. (Reston Pkwy.), Reston,
VA, 703-904-0703
■ The only debate is whether the "great food" at these Tex-
Mex cantinas is worth the "inevitable" wait and "weight";
beyond that there's consensus: the chips and salsa "taste
just made", "everything" from the fajita/burrito standards
to cabrito (goat) and quail specialties is tempting, and
appearance-wise, they do "down-to-earth well."

River Club, The ◑　　　20 | 23 | 19 | $38
3223 K St., NW (bet. Wisconsin Ave. & 32nd St.),
202-333-8118
■ With the revival of interest in dress-up glamour, caviar
and champagne, the "comeback" of this "classy"
Georgetown supper club is cause for celebration; its new
Contemporary Continental menu is a great prelude to big
band dancing (Thursdays) and "power divorcee" romancing;
go for "good dining" and great "time travel."

R.T.'s 🅂　　　24 | 14 | 21 | $27
3804 Mt. Vernon Ave. (Glebe Rd.), Alexandria, VA,
703-684-6010
■ Don't "judge" this joint "by its (seedy) neighborhood",
though much of its loosened-tie appeal comes from
remaining what it always was – an Arlington neighborhood
saloon with "very good New Orleans–style seafood";
presidential patronage hasn't "spoiled" it.

Rupperts
─│─│─│ M
1017 7th St., NW (bet. New York Ave. & L St.), 202-783-0699
This "up-and-coming" Contemporary American on the fringes of Chinatown serves major league food with a minor league tab; by day, it's an NPR (National Public Radio) lunchroom (for the likes of Nina Tottenberg, Leslie Stahl and Cokie Roberts) and at night a hangout for artistic types; get there before everyone else does.

Ruth's Chris Steakhouse S
22 │ 20 │ 21 │ $36
1801 Connecticut Ave., NW (S St.), 202-797-0033
2231 Crystal Dr. (23rd St.), Crystal City, VA, 703-979-7275
■ There's nothing like a "sizzling" juicy steak smothered in butter for that "occasional jolt of cholesterol", and it tastes best served "without haughtiness"; while some feel these straight-ahead steakhouses "lack Morton's polish and The Palm's style", their focus is "great red meat", "good drinks" and Crystal City's "impressive view."

Sabang S
19 │ 18 │ 21 │ $19
2504 Ennalls Ave. (Georgia Ave.), Wheaton, MD, 301-942-7859
◪ Try this "exotic"-looking Wheaton spot for a bargain "cruise" through Indonesia's "interesting" cuisine; its "generous" multicourse rijstaffel is a good place to start, particularly if you go with a group, and modest demands; most find its food a bit "oily" and more than a bit "hot."

Saigon Gourmet S
22 │ 15 │ 20 │ $20
2635 Connecticut Ave., NW (Calvert St.), 202-265-1360
■ Most consider this Woodley Park cafe "the best \Vietnamese in town", though "as with so many good Vietnamese" one "needs to know what to order" (caramel chicken, grilled meats); it's so friendly they "remember you on your second visit", and with its redo finished, its weak spot,"decor, should be improved."

Saigonnais S
─│─│─│ M
2307 18th St., NW (Belmont Rd.), 202-232-5300
A "treasured" Adams Morgan Vietnamese with "yuppie-level food"; its "delicate" French-accented Indochinese dishes are "graciously prepared and served" in a soothing townhouse; a good choice for a "romantic" meal that you hope will never end.

Sakura Palace S
▽ 22 │ 17 │ 20 │ $22
7926 Georgia Ave. (Eastern Ave.), Silver Spring, MD,
301-587-7070
■ The Silver Spring neighborhood has changed for the worse, but this "top-quality" Japanese classic hasn't; it thrives because of its "excellent" sushi and cooked dishes, because its traditional setting and service seem pleasantly "authentic" and because it's a "great bargain at lunch."

Sala Thai [S] — 21 | 15 | 19 | $19

2016 P St., NW (20th St., near Dupont Circle), 202-872-1144

◪ Though its "dark", "stylish" setting can be intriguing for a "low-cost" lunch near Dupont Circle, reactions to this step-down Siamese and its "pungent" food range from "basement eatery but top-floor quality" to "utilitarian" (a minority); N.B. it turns "hectic" at night.

Sam & Harry's — 23 | 22 | 22 | $38

1200 19th St., NW (bet. M & N Sts.), 202-296-4333

■ This "contemporary" version of a "clubby" old-fashioned steakhouse is run like an "attentive private club with no membership fees" or admission policy; it dishes up "first-rate" red meat and "plain" fish at a fancy price, and tries to make everybody "feel like a somebody" (which many are).

Santa Fe East [S] — 22 | 22 | 20 | $25

110 S. Pitt St. (bet. King & Prince Sts.), Alexandria, VA, 703-548-6900

◪ An "intimate" old Santa Fe ambiance is recreated in the courtyards and interior of this historic Alexandria building; in contrast, its kitchen aims at "sophisticated", neo- Southwestern food, exciting when "they get it right", but sometimes "bland" and "heavy"; unfortunately, "one never knows" about its service.

Sarinah Satay House [S] — 20 | 19 | 17 | $21

1338 Wisconsin Ave., NW (bet. N & O Sts.), 202-337-2955

◪ "Tucked away in Georgetown" is a "subterranean", "make-believe" Bali that's fine for a "respite" in a "garden"-like setting and a "different", slow-paced, inexpensive meal, but don't expect more than "nice atmosphere, average food."

Sea Catch — 21 | 21 | 20 | $34

Canal Sq., 1054 31st St., NW (M St.), 202-337-8855

◪ In handsome Georgetown quarters with an "elegant" raw bar and a "delightful" deck "overlooking the canal", this cosmopolitan fish house offers very good seafood that "could be better" for the price; given its strengths, one wonders why it sometimes gets "lonely" here.

SEASONS [S] — 25 | 25 | 25 | $45

Four Seasons Hotel, 2800 Pennsylvania Ave., NW (29th St.), 202-944-2000

■ Its new name may be unfamiliar, but the redecorated Four Seasons hotel dining room is as "lovely and luxurious" as ever – still "perfect for business", yet "not at all stuffy" – and its new Contemporary American menu gets a very high rating; our surveyors "loved it before and after its transformation"; the garden terrace is a "great splurge of a brunch spot."

Sequoia ◑Ⓢ   18 | 24 | 18 | $27 |
3000 K St., NW (Washington Harbour), 202-944-4200
☑ "Spectacular" sunsets and people-watching from its sweeping Washington Harbour terrace, and this "grand ole cruise ship's" dining room, draw huge crowds more interested in "socializing" and sight-seeing than in eating the "non-serious" American food; for eating, it's best at brunch or "grazing"; for spectator sport, go on Friday night.

Sesto Senso Ⓢ   20 | 20 | 19 | $26 |
1214 18th St., NW (bet. M St. & Jefferson Pl.), 202-785-9525
☑ A "high-tech" Italian, below Dupont Circle, with two crowds: one going "for carpaccio", pastas and "veggie dishes" (early and at lunch), the others, for the "oh so loud and smoky", "everyone-has-the-look" Euro scene; both camps complain about discomfort and "pretension", but never about the "beautiful Italian patrons."

701 Ⓢ   23 | 24 | 23 | $35 |
701 Pennsylvania Ave., NW (7th St.), 202-393-0701
■ This lower Pennsylvania Avenue modern American "doesn't get the headlines", but it does get high marks from several hundred surveyors as "an elegant, relaxing restaurant for adults" with "first-class cuisine", "space and privacy" where the "customer matters"; its tapas and the caviar and champagne bar are major winners.

Seven Seas ◑Ⓢ   20 | 11 | 18 | $16 |
Federal Plaza, 1776 E. Jefferson St. (bet. Montrose & Rollins Aves.), Rockville, MD, 301-770-5020
☑ It's said to have "the best Chinese seafood on the East Coast" and its unprepossessing Rockville shopping-strip n yet its staff is "friendly and eager to please" Westerners; however, be sure to "ask for the Chinese" menu or you'll think you "hit a bad day"; N.B. it also offers good sushi.

1789 Ⓢ   24 | 25 | 24 | $42 |
1226 36th St., NW (Prospect St.), 202-965-1789
■"Ambiance plus" some of the best New American food in town make this "civilized" retreat "an excellent choice" for "intimate evenings or out-of-town guests"; it's like dining in a gracious "Georgetown home", only better, and people who haven't eaten here "in years" are "blown away" by the improvement; a bit "pricey", but "you feel good when you leave."

Sfuzzi Ⓢ   19 | 20 | 17 | $26 |
Union Station, 50 Mass. Ave., NE, 202-842-4141
☑ Franchised "Italian verve" and "froufrou dining" in soaring Union Station space; a major Congressional "listening post", many patronize it for "good pastas and drinks", but it can seem "cliquish" with "clueless" help.

Silver Diner ◐ [S] 14 | 17 | 16 | $14

11806 Rockville Pike (bet. Montrose & Old Georgetown Rds.), Rockville, MD, 301-770-2828
14550 Baltimore Ave. (Cherry Ln.), Laurel, MD, 301-470-6080

■ These diner "updates" use "campy" decor, "waitresses with character" and a "retro" menu to convey a '50s "spirit"; most like them best "for breakfast" and "for afters" – "after shopping", "after work", "after movies" and "after hours"; at "kiddie meal times", "pandemonium reigns."

Skewers [S] 21 | 16 | 19 | $19

1633 P St., NW (bet. 16th & 17th Sts.), 202-387-7400

■ Very popular Mediterranean near Dupont Circle that "never takes its customers for granted"; that, as much as its "healthy", "reliable menu" and low prices, is its appeal; it's an informal living room for local intelligentsia, "intensely mellow" and always interesting; ditto the "lunar" downstairs coffee bar/cafe.

Southside 815 [S] 18 | 15 | 17 | $20

815 S. Washington St. (bet. Franklin & Green Sts.), Alexandria, VA, 703-836-6222

■ A promising young Alexandrian brings "originality" and "gourmet ingredients" to traditional Southern cooking, but isn't "inventive" enough to make the calories disappear; this unfancy neighborhood spot is getting area-wide attention, which strains service and space, but still "everyone wants to go back."

Starke's Head Hog BBQ [S] – | – | – | I

(aka George Starke's Head Hog BBQ)

7003 Wisconsin Ave. (Walsh St.), Bethesda, MD, 301-907-9110

The Boss Hog's BBQ, a 'Skins shrine in a newly minted Bethesda small town diner where everything that's not burgundy and gold is covered with memorabilia; still, we hear the pit stuff ain't half bad, lean and piled hog high with crispy sides, and down-home blues scoring in the background.

Star of Siam [S] 18 | 14 | 16 | $18

1136 19th St., NW (bet. L & M Sts.), 202-785-2838
2446 18th St., NW (Columbia Rd.), 202-986-4133
International Pl., 1735 N. Lynn St. (N. 19th St.), Rosslyn, VA, 703-524-1208

◪ Favored by fire-eaters for their "extra hot" spicing and "affordable" pricing, these Thais vary greatly by location; the 19th Street townhouse is a "top lunch spot for a quiet meeting"; in Adams Morgan, it's rooftop chic, while Rosslyn is strictly a neighborhood Thai with "better choices" nearby.

State of the Union [S] – | – | – | I
1357 U St. (bet. 13th & 14th Sts.), 202-588-8810
This young, "hip" New Uer is on the fringe geographically, culturally and culinarily; it serves "surprisingly good and cheap" Russian food in romantically dark, avant-garde grunge; even if you can't tell a pierogi from a potato chip, check out the "great bar" scene and the witty 'no-more-Cold-War-anymore' decor.

Steamers [S] ▽ 15 | 10 | 14 | $19
4820 Auburn Ave. (Norfolk Ave.), Bethesda, MD, 301-718-0661
◪ It's a great idea – recreate a "beachlike", kick-back casual, smash-those-crabs, drink-beer and make-noise crabshack in convenient Bethesda; though this tent-top is "mostly a summer sensation", its "inexpensive" fun.

Stella's [S] – | – | – | M
1725 Duke St. (across from King St. Metro Sta.), Alexandria, VA, 703-519-1946
In Alexandria, this moderately priced '40s flashback is proving that juicy burgers and chops, "greasy fried" onion rings, and rich, "delicious desserts" are just as irresistible now as they were before cholesterol was invented; wonderful memorabilia (photos, artifacts and models), "big-band-theme" sound track and outdoor patio add appeal.

Straits of Malaya [S] 23 | 19 | 19 | $21
1836 18th St., NW (T St.), 202-483-1483
◪ A very good place to sample Singapore and Malaysian cuisines, this appealing Asian's seasonally changing menu "rewards the adventurous" and its "veranda-like" dining room and "tropical treehouse" roof deck are two of the nicest places to eat in Adams Morgan; service and sometimes even the kitchen can "fall apart", but "it's worth" taking your chances.

Sunny Garden [S] ▽ 21 | 10 | 18 | $15
1302 E. Gude Dr. (S. Law Rd.), Rockville, MD, 301-762-7477
■ The Chinese menu is pink, and it's unusually "interesting", at this "almost-too-out-of-the-way" Rockville Taiwanese; although it looks like another kid-proof "Formica" stop with "friendly" help and very cheap prices, it tastes, "surprisingly", like one of the area's "best."

Sushi-Ko [S] 23 | 15 | 19 | $25
2309 Wisconsin Ave., NW (south of Calvert St.), 202-333-4187
■ Sushi fit for the emperor of Japan can be sampled at this "faded" Glover Park sushi bar; it's "where local and visiting Japanese go" and it catered the royal visit; our surveyors come here for its "innovative" choices, noodle soups, "affordable prices" and "fast service."

Tabard Inn S　　　　21 | 21 | 20 | $27 |
Tabard Inn, 1739 N St., NW (bet. 17th & 18th Sts.),
202-833-2668
■ There are few more "charming places for a rendezvous"
than this "tattered hotel" near Dupont Circle; brunch in its
"lovely" summer courtyard, or "collapsing" on the "old
couches" by the fireplace evoke romantic memories; the
Eclectic food is sometimes "more trendy than tasty", but
that doesn't concern most reviewers.

TABERNA DEL ALABARDERO　　　25 | 26 | 25 | $43 |
1776 I St., NW (18th St.), 202-429-2200
■ If you've never been to Spain, you may be surprised to
find earthy, "sensational olive oil and garlic flavors in
beautiful surroundings", yet that's what makes this elegant
Downtown restaurant so "like Madrid"; many aficionados
consider it "the most sophisticated dining in the area" with
"stellar" food and service, plus "unsurpassed" tapas —
that is, "if money is no object."

Tachibana　　　　24 | 16 | 21 | $25 |
4050 Lee Hwy. (Military Rd.), Arlington, VA, 703-528-1122
■ According to many sushi-lovers, you "can't ask for
anything more" than "consistently" fresh, clean, well-
made specimens "at a reasonable price"; if so, this Arlington
Japanese offers the "best sushi for the money plus "lots
of other interesting (and even cheaper) choices", which
explains why it's often "crowded" and "rushed."

Taipei/Tokyo Cafe S　　　18 | 5 | 9 | $11 |
Metro Ctr. Plaza, 11510-A Rockville Pike (Nicholson Ln.),
Rockville, MD, 301-881-8388
◪ Don't even bother stopping at this Rockville Asian
storefront "unless you're hungry", because when you order
a bowl of steaming "homemade" noodle soup, you really
get a meal; it's a "no-nonsense, no-decor" cafeteria-style
place with not enough tables, a "limited choice" of "very
fresh sushi" and "good value" Chinese food.

Tako Grill　　　　23 | 18 | 19 | $22 |
7756 Wisconsin Ave. (Cheltenham Rd.), Bethesda, MD,
301-652-7030
■ Slightly offbeat, this Bethesda storefront "copies Tokyo
grills" by serving a "smorgasbord of Japanese dishes",
including sushi, robata (stone-hearth grills) and noodle
soups; go with a group and "mix and match", expect waits
(no reserving), "picnic-table atmosphere" and somewhat
weak service.

Tara Thai [S] – | – | – | M

226 Maple Ave. W. (bet. Lawyer's Rd. & Nutley St.), Vienna, VA, 703-255-2467

This suburban takeoff on Busara's high-tech, gloss-and-modern Thai food has "become the hottest restaurant in Fairfax so fast" that its new fans just "hope they keep up the quality" and "super service."

Taste of Saigon [S] 24 | 20 | 22 | $18

410 Hungerford Dr. (Beall Ave.), Rockville, MD, 301-424-7222

■ An "excellent" example of why "family-run is always best", this Rockville Vietnamese offers "adventurous", flavorful food and a "visually appealing" setting; it's "convenient" for "everyday occasions" and a "relaxed" place for a low-cost business lunch served by the family.

Taverna Cretekou [S] 21 | 20 | 20 | $25

818 King St. (bet. Alfred & Columbus Sts.), Alexandria, VA, 703-548-8688

■ The "arbored garden" of this Old Town taverna, and its festive weekend dinners, are the time-honored way locals visit Greece without a passport; less celebrated is the recent addition of uncommon and healthful regional dishes to its repertoire of Greek standards.

Tavola [S] 22 | 20 | 19 | $26

710 King St. (Columbus St.), Alexandria, VA, 703-683-9070

■ Not as rosy, but just as good – Terrazza's downscaled annex is "bright and light" with "a warm welcome"; its antipasti cart is all the decoration the white room really needs since the "fine bread", pasta and seafood are the same high quality as its sister, though more sensibly portioned and at two-thirds the price.

Tempo [S] ▽ 24 | 16 | 21 | $26

4231 Duke St. (N. Gordon St.), Alexandria, VA, 703-370-7900

■ An "unlikely location" in a "converted Alexandria garage" may explain why this cramped "hectic" Italian bistro feels like a "find"; its "imaginative" pastas, "superb" fish and Southwestern-influenced specials have endeared it to the "neighborhood" as a "diamond in the rough."

Terramar [S] 22 | 22 | 21 | $26

7800 Wisconsin Ave. (Cheltenham Dr.), Bethesda, MD, 301-654-0888

◪ A fountain courtyard creates a pleasing Latin backdrop for sharing tapas at this "accommodating" Bethesda Nicaraguan; while it serves Central American specialties, "meat-and-potato types" feel "comfortable" with the "solid" food; however, according to a few more-demanding diners, nit "needs something extra to make it worth the price."

Terrazza [S] 22 | 22 | 21 | $36
710 King St. (bet. Washington & Columbus Sts.), Alexandria, VA, 703-683-6900
◪ The top of the line in Old Town; for many, its flower-filled "elegance" and skillful "use of fresh ingredients" in "Italian cuisine à la française" are worth a premium, especially on "special occasions"; happily, with scaled-down versions of the same food for less money at Tavola next door, diners have a choice.

T.G.I. Friday's ◐ [S] 14 | 14 | 15 | $15
4650 King St. (N. Beauregard St.), Alexandria, VA, 703-931-4101
12147 Rockville Pike (Twinbrook Pkwy.), Rockville, MD, 301-231-9048
6460 Capitol Dr. (Greenbelt Rd.), Greenbelt, MD, 301-345-2503, 2504
13071 Worldgate Dr. (Elden St.), Herndon, VA, 703-787-9630
2070 Chain Bridge Rd. (Old Courthouse Rd.), Tysons Corner, VA, 703-556-6160
2100 Pennsylvania Ave. (21st St., NW), 202-872-4344
1201 Pennsylvania Ave. (1 block north of Federal Triangle Metro Station), 202-628-8443
7401 Sudley Rd. (Nicholson St.), Manassas, VA, 703-330-8333
14600 Baltimore Ave. (Cherry Ln.), Laurel, MD, 301-498-8443
13225 Worth Ave. (across from Potomac Mills), Woodbridge, VA, 703-492-0090
◪ This fern bar 'n' burger chain is a "kid favorite", holds "hyper" happy hours and gives execs "a place to take their secretaries" for lunch; for what they are – "fallback restaurants" – they meet expectations: "always slow", "fun", "loud", "crowded" and serving "something for everyone", most of it fried.

Thai Flavor [S] ▽ 21 | 15 | 20 | $19
3228 Wisconsin Ave. (Macomb St.), 202-966-0200
■ Installed in vaguely "Victorian" Upper Wisconsin Avenue quarters is one of the "best Thais around" with "well-spiced", yet refined, Chinese-influenced food and a staff that "become old friends by the third trip"; unlike many pseudo-bargain spreads, its buffet lunch is really "wonderful."

Thai Kingdom [S] 22 | 19 | 20 | $20
2021 K St., NW (bet. 20th & 21st Sts.), 202-835-1700
■ In lawyerland, this K Street Thai is "lunch-bargain" territory, yet it's "dependable, friendly" and "delicious" enough to make staying in DC for "dinner attractive"; true, the "overdone" decor "looks corny, but it's like that in Thailand", too.

Thai Place 🅢
20 | 13 | 19 | $17 |
*4828 Cordell Ave. (Woodmont Ave.), Bethesda, MD,
301-951-0535*
☑ Many of those who were introduced to Thai food at this
worn-down Bethesda family place keep coming back
because it's "reliable", "cheap" and friendly, and it makes
their favorite dishes in its "old-style" way; no decor makes
carryout the "better" option.

Thai Taste 🅢
20 | 15 | 17 | $17 |
2606 Connecticut Ave., NW (Calvert St.), 202-387-8876
☑ There's wonderful outdoor people-watching and some
very good, "very affordable" Thai dishes (crispy whole fish,
green curry, Thai salad) at this Woodley-Park old-timer; the
trick is to enjoy them "before they push you out the door."

That's Amore 🅢
19 | 16 | 20 | $23 |
*15201 Shady Grove Rd. (Research Blvd.), Rockville, MD,
301-670-9666
Danor Plaza, 150 Branch Rd. (Rte. 123), Vienna, VA,
703-281-7777*
☑ You "gotta go en masse" with no "picky eaters", "parties
of two" or garlic-phobes to these boisterous family-style
Italian feederies; everyone shares "gargantuan" platters
of old-fashioned, heavy-duty food in campy "*Godfather*
settings": it's almost impossible not to overeat.

Tia Queta 🅢
20 | 16 | 20 | $21 |
*8009 Norfolk Ave. (Old Georgetown Rd.), Bethesda, MD,
301-654-4443*
■ A Mexican you "can get into" near Rio Grande Cafe,
this colorful cantina has attractions that go beyond its open
door and outdoor space, such as "real" Mexican country
cooking featuring "more seafood, less spice", a "great
chicken mole" and making an "honest effort" to please.

Tiberio
22 | 21 | 20 | $45 |
1915 K St., NW (bet. 19th & 20th Sts.), 202-452-1915
☑"You're either a fan or not" of this legendary "expense-
account" Northern Italian, and most "are" – for its elegance,
very helpful staff and "melt-in-your-mouth" pasta and veal;
and they remain fans notwithstanding gags about prices:
"tax shelter for pasta", "refinance your home first."

Tivoli
22 | 22 | 22 | $31 |
1700 N. Moore St. (19th St.), Rosslyn, VA, 703-524-8900
■ "Elegance and courtesy" are the "hallmarks" of this
"lovely, professionally run, old-line restaurant" in Rosslyn
with a Northern Italian–Continental menu, "outstanding"
desserts and a bill that's "less than expected"; it's a
"great place for business lunches" and "sophisticated
brunches", yet people too often "forget about this place."

Tomato Palace, The S   ▽ 21 | 19 | 20 | $19
10221 Wincopin Circle (Rte. 175), Columbia, MD, 410-715-0211
■ "Bellissimo!", Columbia neighbors bless this lighthearted, lakeside bistro as the "best thing that ever happened", family dining-wise; its homey, hearty "Newark-Italian" pizzas, pastas and platters are "done with the best ingredients and intentions" for a "modest" price – and its Trenton tomato pie has done more for New Jersey than the Giants or even Governor Whitman.

Tom Tom S   – | – | – | M
2333 18th St. NW (bet. Belmont St. & Kalorama Rd.), 202-588-1300
A frenetic beat drives Adams Morgan's hottest place, an open-to-the-street, multilevel culturama where artists create works in progress (on elevated platforms) and everyone else sips sangria slushes, sups on clever Mediterranean tapas, pizzas, pastas and grills, and checks out the stars (from the rooftop deck) and each other; prices peak at $10.

Tony and Joe's Seafood Place S   16 | 18 | 16 | $27
Washington Harbour, 3000 K St., NW (30th St.), 202-944-4545
☑ This Washington Harbour "fishbowl" gets top marks for riverside terrace views, and "you can't beat the outside bar" for Friday night singling (it's "nothing special" inside); judgments of the seafood and service veer from "great" to "so-so", but in nice weather everyone seems to go.

Tony Cheng's Seafood S   19 | 16 | 17 | $20
Tony Cheng's Mongolian S
619 H St., NW (bet. 6th & 7th Sts.), 202-842-TONY
☑ Downstairs it's all-you-can-eat dining with a Mongolian twist (choose ingredients to be stir-fried, grilled or steeped tableside in hot-pots) at this Chinatown "must for over-40 Midwesterners" and hungry kids; upstairs, it serves "very good dim sum" and seafood; N.B. be careful at night.

TooJay's S   16 | 10 | 14 | $15
4620 Wisconsin Ave., NW (Chesapeake St.), 202-686-1989
☑ A "gloomy", Upper NW "Jewish-style noshery" "where NYers find each other", along with an "approximation" of the corned beef, pastrami and heartburn of their youth; since the "service is surly and sandwiches are stuffed", most settle to skip a trip on the Shuttle.

Tortilla Coast S   16 | 15 | 16 | $16
201 Mass. Ave., NE (D St.), 202-546-6768
☑ Loud and "brash" like the Senate interns socializing in its frontyard (or the "black" hole inside) while snarfing down margaritas and "free chips" (dinner on "a Hill salary"); rumor has it that this Tex-Mex's kitchen has "improved" but some remain skeptical or simply "have outgrown it."

Tortilla Factory [S] 20 | 13 | 18 | $14

The Pines, 648 Elden St. (Monroe St.), Herndon, VA, 703-471-1156

◪ Is this outer-suburban Tex-Mex standby a "diamond in the grass" and "worth the drive to Herndon" or just a "hole-in-the-wall, not worth the wait" for a family fill-up? well, it's "cheap", "quick", uses "fresh ingredients", has "good veggie options" and "addictive" salsa, and is a rare "lunch place in the middle of nowhere."

Tragara [S] 22 | 22 | 21 | $40

4935 Cordell Ave. (bet. Old Georgetown Rd. & Norfolk Ave.), Bethesda, MD, 301-951-4935

◪ What keeps this posh Northern Italian from getting "lost" in Bethesda's restaurant-dense, 'Woodmont Triangle' is its reputation for "elegance" (some say "glitz"), "solicitous" ("snippy") service, "pasta-perfect" dining and the Rolls pulling up in front; the real question is, will it outlast its monied clientele ("average age 65")?

Trattu 22 | 19 | 21 | $26

1823 Jefferson Pl., NW (bet. Connecticut Ave. & 19th St.), 202-466-4570

■ Everything about this unpretentious Dupont Circle trattoria is the "perfect antidote to power dining"; it looks a "little the worse for wear", its menu of "hearty", garlicky pastas, seafood and veal defies trends, and seating is too "tight" for confidences; however, its devotees "wouldn't change a thing", especially the prices.

Trumpets [S] 24 | 21 | 22 | $27

1603 17th St., NW (Q St.), 202-232-4141

■ "Past the gay bar" of this Dupont Circle East spot is a back dining room serving "cutting-edge" Contemporary American food to a "very urban mix"; its "funky, modern" underground decor suits the "eclectic" food and somewhat "fussy" presentation; brunch is a good time to share this "inside secret."

Tung Bor [S] 18 | 14 | 16 | $19

4819 St. Elmo Ave. (bet. Woodmont Ave. & Old Georgetown Rd.), Bethesda, MD, 301-656-3883

◪ Bunkered in Bethesda, at *Survey*-time this dim sum palace was adjusting to its new location: it still looks "like a warehouse", "crowded and noisy", if no longer shabby, and still rolls out sometimes "super" daily dim sum; reviews on the rest of the extensive menu and the "dour" waiters are mixed.

Tuscana West ◐ ▽ 19 20 17 $26
1350 I St., NW (bet. 13th & 14th Sts.), 202-289-7300
◪ This glossy, "new Italian rave" in lawyerland pushes trendy buttons like "brick-oven pizza", "creative" pasta, "grilled choices" and open kitchen – it's having its moment, but some are extremely "not impressed", or, as they say on the Internet, "flame it."

Two Quail [S] 22 23 22 $28
320 Mass. Ave., NE (bet. 3rd & 4th Sts.), 202-543-8030
◪ An endearing Capitol Hill jumble of mix-and-matched Victoriana and New American menu concoctions like "crab latkes with rapscallion sauce" is variously described as "quirky", "funky", "comfy", "romantic" and "quaint"; a handful of critics say: "like the decor in my attic better"; "Nouvelle Rehoboth Beach cuisine."

Union Street Public House [S] 19 19 18 $19
121 S. Union St. (bet. King & Prince Sts.), Alexandria, VA, 703-548-1785
■ With "tons of character", bar food that "consistently" tastes "good" and the "best selection" of microbrews on tap, this "classic" Old Town saloon hosts a lively singles scene; it's also a "sunny", "comfortable" setting for families with sandwiches, Southern seafood and service that seems like they "made it just for you", but not always on busy weekends.

Veneziano ◐ [S] 22 18 21 $27
2305 18th St., NW (Kalorama Rd.), 202-483-9300
■ If Adams Morgan is your "part of town", this very "professional" North Italian needs no introduction; its "vera cucina veneta" is as "authentic" as its warm "reception", while its early-bird/late-supper $13.95 menu brings some "unusual" dishes in bargain-dining range; a few caution that "it's not as good as all that."

VIDALIA 24 22 22 $35
1990 M St., NW (bet. 19th & 20th Sts.), 202-659-1990
◪ Native and born-again "Southerners stand up and applaud" this "Nu-Vo (sic), as they say back home", Southern bistro with a "fresh new approach" to regional food; critics are kind: "hits and misses with a drawl"; "hope for a decent waiter."

Vietnam Georgetown [S] 19 13 16 $21
2934 M St., NW (30th St.), 202-337-4536
◪ This Vietnamese veteran has held up its M Street corner "for so long" it seems "more G'town than Nam" to locals, though not to tourists who like it for "decent" meals that make "only a small dent in your wallet"; its patio, "crispy rolls" and fresh seafood are more than "adequate."

Vincenzo and Trattoria "al Sole" S   24 | 22 | 21 | $41
1606 20th St., NW (bet. Q St. & Connecticut Ave.),
202-667-0047
■ Long "unequaled" for polished service and fresh seafood
"cooked to perfection", this "elegant" Northern Italian
near Dupont Circle has even more appeal thanks to a new
(post-*Survey*) trattoria format and lower-priced menu at
"al Sole" (downstairs); upstairs, in a boutique dining room,
V still serves its trademark "classical" cuisine for dinner.

Volare S   – | – | – | M
(fka La Taverna d'Italia)
4926 St. Elmo Ave. (bet. Old Georgetown Rd. & Norfolk
Ave.), Bethesda, MD, 301-907-7503
☑ Apart from a new name (reflecting changed ownership),
this is still just a "nice"-looking, overcrowded, neighborhood
restaurant serving pastas, fish and veal "without hoopla",
and not the "classy, affordable Italian" Bethesda allegedly
"needs"; despite "some great dishes" (notably the fish
soup), this place has never taken off.

Warehouse Bar & Grill S   21 | 20 | 20 | $26
214 King St. (bet. Fairfax & Lee Sts.), Alexandria, VA,
703-683-6868
■ An Alexandria waterfront "favorite" with an upscale
business-lunch and "bar scene"; it serves some of Old
Town's "freshest seafood" and is "one of the few places
to get a steak" thereabouts, along with Creole cooking
that reflects its sibling, R.T.'s.

West End Cafe ◐ S   20 | 20 | 19 | $28
1 Washington Circle Hotel, NW (New Hampshire Ave.),
202-293-5390
■ Washingtonians don't think of this "very intime" West
Ender as a hotel restaurant, they use it so much; it's "a
favorite before or after Kennedy Center" because there's
free limo service and the light, if "chancy", Californian
cuisine doesn't make you "stuffed"; later the "best hostess"
and the "best" piano player pull "a good crowd."

WILLARD ROOM S   24 | 27 | 24 | $46
Willard Hotel, 1401 Pennsylvania Ave., NW (bet. 14th &
15th Sts.), 202-637-7440
■ DC's showplace, this "magnificent" Victorian dining
room reeks "old money" ("robber baron") elegance and
"courtliness"; just being there makes guests "feel well-
fed and pampered"; although its Euro-American food has
always been "excellent", the arrival of talented new-chef
Guy Reinbolt means it could soar.

Willow Grove Inn [S] 💳̸ ▽ 27 | 26 | 25 | $37

Willow Grove Inn, 14079 Plantation Way (off Rte. 15, 1 mile north of Orange), Orange, VA, 703-672-5982

■ A beautifully restored antebellum mansion near Charlottesville, that's "perfect" for "an idyllic garden meal"; watching the moon rise in such a setting "makes everything taste good", but even inside the Regional American food is "outstanding", producing many "memorable experiences."

Woo Lae Oak [S] 22 | 17 | 17 | $24

River House, 1500 S. Joyce St., Arlington, VA, 703-521-3706

◪ "Real Korea! foodwise" in Arlington – it's the biggest and most attractive local place to try this very "spicy fare", with tabletop BBQ for "smoky" group grilling along with "authentic" soups, noodle dishes and casseroles; if possible, go with "someone who is known and knows what to order"; P.S. English is the staff's second language.

Wurzburg-Haus 20 | 15 | 19 | $20

Red Mill Shopping Ctr., 7236 Muncaster Mill Rd. (Shady Grove Rd.), Rockville, MD, 301-330-0402

■ It may seem faster to fly to Germany than to drive to this kitschy "Gasthaus" in Gaithersburg, but it's "cheerful" and cheap, and the "beer, bread, spaetzle and cabbage" are so good and so filling you may never get to the "robust" entrees and terrific desserts; go "before 5 PM" to avoid the lines – pretend it's a "late lunch."

Yosaku [S] 21 | 15 | 20 | $22

4712 Wisconsin Ave., NW (bet. Chesapeake & Davenport Sts.), 202-363-4453

◪ Among the reasons why "people love this" Upper NW Japanese are its "excellent" prices for first-rate sushi and a great "variety" of other dishes, "convenience" for movies, shopping and on-the-way-home stops, and "gracious" management; its decor is less appealing, but don't be misled.

INDEXES TO WASHINGTON, D.C. RESTAURANTS

SPECIAL FEATURES AND APPEALS

TYPES OF CUISINE

Afghan
Bamiyan
Kabul Caravan
Panjshir

American (Contemporary)
Allegro
American Cafe
Belmont Kitchen
Bistro Bistro
Bistro 2015
Bleu Rock Inn
Boss Cats
Cafe BaBaLu
Cafe Bethesda
Cafe Pierre
Carlyle Grand Cafe
Celadon
Chardonnay
Cities
Coeur de Lion
Collector, The
Colonnade, The
Dean & DeLuca Cafe
Elysium
Fedora Cafe
Fleetwood's
4 & 20 Blackbirds
Garden Cafe
Georgia Brown's
Imperial Hotel
Inn at Glen Echo
Inn/Little Wash.
Jefferson
Kinkead's
Lafayette
Le Bon Cafe
Little Fountain Cafe
Madeo
Melrose
Metro Center Grille
Morrison-Clark Inn
Mrs. Simpson's
New Heights
Nicholas
Nora
Old Angler's Inn
Oval Room
Peasant Rest.
Perry's
Pesce
Planet Hollywood
Pleasant Peasant

Rupperts
Seasons
Sequoia
701
1789
T.G.I. Friday's
Trumpets
Two Quail
Vidalia
West End Cafe
Willard Room
Willow Grove Inn

American (Regional)
Cafe Pierre
Cities
Frog & the Redneck
Garden Cafe
Inn/Little Wash.
Jefferson
Lafayette
Madeo
Old Angler's Inn
1789
West End Cafe
Willow Grove Inn

American (Traditional)
America
Artie's
Belmont Kitchen
Bilbo Baggins
Bistro Bistro
Bob & Edith's
Calvert Grille
Capitol City Brew
Carlyle Grand Cafe
Carnegie Deli
C.F. Folks
Chadwicks
Chart House
Cheesecake Factory
Clyde's
Coventry Cross
Evans Farm Inn
Florida Ave. Grill
Fleetwood's
Foggy Bottom Cafe
Gangplank
Gary's
Georgetown Grill
Geppetto
Grill, RC, Pent.

Guards
Gulf Coast Kitchen
Hamburger Hamlet
Hard Rock Cafe
Hard Times Cafe
Herb's
Hogate's
Houlihan's
Houston's
J. Paul's
Kramerbooks
Martin's Tavern
Mick's
Mike's Amer. Grill
Monocle
Montgomery's Grille
Music City Roadhouse
Occidental Grill
O'Donnell's
Old Ebbitt Grill
Phillips Flagship
Pier 7
Polly's Cafe
Potowmack Landing
Prime Rib
Ruth's Chris
Sam & Harry's
Sequoia
Silver Diner
Southside 815
State of the Union
Stella's
T.G.I. Friday's
Union St. Public Hse.
Warehouse Grill

Bakeries
Firehook Bakery
la Madeleine
Palais du Chocolat
Patisserie Didier

Bar-B-Q
Capitol City Brew
Chicken Place
Clyde's
Crisp & Juicy
Head's
Houston's
Mick's
O'Brien's
Old Ebbitt Grill
Old Glory BBQ
Red Hot & Blue
Starke's BBQ

Brazilian
Coco Loco
Grill from Ipanema

Cajun/Creole
Cajun Bangkok
Louisiana Express
Lulu's
R.T.'s
Warehouse Grill

Caribbean
Cafe Atlantico
Hibiscus Cafe
Montego Cafe

Chinese
China Canteen
China Chef
China Inn
City Lights of China
Eat First
Foong Lin
Fortune
Four Rivers
Full Kee
Good Fortune
House of Chinese
Hsian Foong
Hunan Chinatown
Hunan Lion
Hunan Manor
Hunan Number One
Jade Palace
Mr. K's
Mr. Yung's
Peking Gourmet
Seven Seas
Sunny Garden
Taipei/Tokyo Cafe
Tony Cheng's
Tung Bor

Continental
Baron's
Falls Landing
Grill, RC, Pent.
Jockey Club
Kazan
Lite 'n' Fair
Powerscourt
Restaurant, RC, Tysons
River Club
Tivoli
Willard Room

Delis
Carnegie Deli
Cafe Mozart
TooJay's

Dim Sum
China Canteen
China Chef
China Inn
Fortune
Four Rivers
Good Fortune
House of Chinese
Hunan Lion
Hunan Number One
Mr. Yung's
Seven Seas
Sunny Garden
Taipei/Tokyo Cafe
Tony Cheng's
Tung Bor

Diners
Bob & Edith's
Florida Ave. Grill
Silver Diner

Eclectic
C.F. Folks
Collector, The
Fern St. Bistro
Planet Hollywood
Tabard Inn

Ethiopian
Meskerem
Red Sea

French Bistro
Bistro Bravo
Bistro Français
Bistro Le Monde
Cafe Bethesda
Gaby's
La Brasserie
La Chaumiere
La Colline
La Cote d'Or
La Fourchette
la Madeleine
La Miche
Lavandou
Le Bon Cafe
Le Caprice
Le Gaulois
Le Mistral

Le Refuge
Les Halles
Palladin
Patisserie Didier
Pesce

French Classic
Jean-Michel
La Bergerie
La Bonne Auberge
La Brasserie
La Chaumiere
La Cote d'Or
La Ferme
La Miche
La Mirabelle
L'Auberge Ch. Francois
L'Auberge Provencale
Le Gaulois
Le Lion d'Or
Le Rivage
Le Vieux Logis
Marquis de Rochambeau
Palladin

French (New)
Bangkok Gourmet
Citronelle
Gerard's Place
Jean-Louis
Jean-Michel
Le Bon Cafe
Le Caprice
Maison Blanche
Provence

German
Cafe Berlin
Cafe Mozart
Wurzburg-Haus

Greek
Alekos
Mykonos
Taverna Cretekou

Hamburgers
Artie's
Bistro Bistro
Boss Cats
Capitol City Brew
Carlyle Grand Cafe
Chadwicks
Clyde's
Coventry Cross
Guards

Perry's
Sakura Palace
Sushi-Ko
Tachibana
Tako Grill
Taipei/Tokyo Cafe
Yosaku

Korean
Ichiban
Woo Lae Oak

Latin
Chicken Place
Coco Loco
Crisp & Juicy
El Caribe
Havana Cafe
Lauriol Plaza
Terramar

Mediterranean
BeDuCi
Eye St. Cafe
Iron Gate
Pasha Cafe
Provence
Skewers
Tom Tom

Mexican/Salvadoran
Atlacatl
Austin Grill
Coco Loco
El Tamarindo
Enriqueta's
Jaimalito's
Lauriol Plaza
Mixtec
Tia Queta
Tortilla Factory

Middle Eastern
Bacchus
Dfouny
Fes
Food Factory
Kazan
Lebanese Taverna
Nizam's
Pasha Cafe
Persepolis

Moroccan
Fes

Pizza
Bertucci's
Cafe Milano
Cafe Petitto
Calif. Pizza Kit.
Coppi's
Ecco Cafe
Faccia Luna
Fleetwood's
Generous George's
Geppetto
Il Forno
Il Radicchio
I Matti
Ledo Pizza
Listrani's
Notte Luna
Paolo's
Pasta Place
Pasta Plus
Pizzeria Paradiso
Tomato Palace
Tom Tom
Tuscana West

Russian
State of the Union

Seafood
Blue Point Grill
Cafe Bethesda
Chart House
Chesapeake Seafood
Clyde's
Crisfield
Falls Landing
Gangplank
Gary's
Georgetown Seafood
Geranio
Hogate's
Jockey Club
J. Paul's
Kinkead's
Le Rivage
Martin's Tavern
Nicholas
O'Donnell's
Palm, The
Phillips Flagship
Pier 7
Potowmack Landing
R.T.'s
Sam & Harry's
Sea Catch

Sequoia
Steamers
Prime Rib
Restaurant, RC, Tysons
Tempo
Tony & Joe's
Tony Cheng's
Vincenzo
Warehouse Grill

SE Asian
Asia Nora
Burma
Germaine's
Lite 'n' Fair
Pan Asian Noodles
Straits of Malaya

Southern
Calvert Grille
Dixie Grill
Florida Ave. Grill
Georgia Brown's
Gulf Coast Kitchen
Head's
Morrison-Clark Inn
Music City Roadhouse
Southside 815
Union St. Public Hse.
Vidalia

Southwestern
Anita's
Armadilla Grill
Austin Grill
Cafe BaBaLu
Cottonwood Cafe
Gabriel
Hard Times Cafe
Jaimalito's
Red Sage
Santa Fe East
Tempo

Spanish
Andalucia
Gabriel
Jaleo
Lauriol Plaza
Taberna del Alabardero
Terramar

Steakhouses
Chart House
Gary's
Guards

Les Halles
Morton's of Chicago
Outback Stkhse.
Palm, The
Prime Rib
Ruth's Chris
Sam & Harry's

Sushi
Ginza's
Sushi-Ko

Tapas
(Best of many)
Cafe Atlantico
Cafe BaBaLu
Coco Loco
Gabriel
Jaleo
Kinkead's
Provence
Terramar
Tom Tom

Tex-Mex
Anita's
Austin Grill
Cactus Cantina
Rio Grande Cafe
Tortilla Coast
Tortilla Factory

Thai
Bangkok Gourmet
Bangkok Orchid
Bua
Busara
Cajun Bangkok
Crystal Thai
Duangrat's
Dusit
Ivy's Place
Pan Asian Noodles
Pilin Thai
Rabieng
Sala Thai
Star of Siam
Tara Thai
Thai Flavor
Thai Kingdom
Thai Place
Thai Taste

Vietnamese
Atami
Cafe Dalat

NEIGHBORHOOD LOCATIONS

WASHINGTON, D.C.

Capitol Hill
American Cafe
Bangkok Orchid
Bistro Le Monde
Head's
La Brasserie
La Colline
Le Bon Cafe
Le Mistral
Monocle
Powerscourt
Sfuzzi
Tortilla Coast
Two Quail

Chinatown/Convention Center/New Downtown
Burma
Capitol City Brew
China Inn
Coco Loco
Eat First
Full Kee
Hard Rock Cafe
Hunan Chinatown
Luigino
Metro Center Grille
Mr. Yung's
Rupperts
State of the Union
Tony Cheng's

Columbia Road/ Adams Morgan
Belmont Kitchen
Bua
Cafe Atlantico
Cities
El Tamarindo
Florida Ave. Grill
Grill from Ipanema
Il Radicchio
I Matti
La Fourchette
Lauriol Plaza
Lebanese Taverna
Little Fountain Cafe
Meskerem
Miss Saigon
Mixtec

Montego Cafe
Perry's
Red Sea
Saigonnais
Star of Siam
Straits of Malaya
Tom Tom
Trumpets
Veneziano

Downtown
Allegro
America
American Cafe
BICE
Bombay Club
Cafe Mozart
Celadon
Chardonnay
Coeur de Lion
Coppi's
Dean & DeLuca Cafe
Dixie Grill
Georgia Brown's
Gerard's Place
Herb's
Jaleo
Jefferson
Lafayette
Les Halles
Maison Blanche
Mick's
Morrison-Clark Inn
Nicholas
Notte Luna
Occidental Grill
Old Ebbitt Grill
Oval Room
Pan Asian Noodles
Peasant Rest.
Planet Hollywood
Polly's Cafe
Red Sage
701
T.G.I. Friday's
Tuscana West
Willard Room

NEARBY MARYLAND

Tragara
Tung Bor
Volare

Gaithersburg

Hamburger Hamlet
Ichiban
Il Forno
Ledo Pizza
Outback Stkhse.
Red Hot & Blue

Rockville

Andalucia
Bombay Bistro
Cheesecake Factory
China Canteen
Crisp & Juicy
Four Rivers
Hard Times Cafe
House of Chinese
Houston's
Il Pizzico
la Madeleine
Ledo Pizza
O'Brien's
Paolo's
Seven Seas
Silver Diner
Sunny Garden
Taipei/Tokyo Cafe
Taste of Saigon

T.G.I. Friday's
That's Amore
Wurzburg-Haus

Silver Spring/Wheaton/ Langley Park/Laurel/ Landover

Calif. Pizza Kit.
Chadwicks
Chicken Place
China Chef
Crisfield
Crisp & Juicy
Dusit
Full Kee
Good Fortune
Ledo Pizza
Nam's
Pasta Plus
Pho 75
Red Hot & Blue
Sabang
Sakura Palace
Silver Diner
T.G.I. Friday's

Chestertown

Imperial Hotel

Columbia

Clyde's
Hunan Manor
Tomato Palace

NEARBY VIRGINIA

Alexandria

Austin Grill
Bamiyan
Bilbo Baggins
Blue Point Grill
Cajun Bangkok
Calvert Grille
Chadwicks
Chart House
Dfouny
East Wind
Elysium
Ecco Cafe
Firehook Bakery
Fleetwood's
Generous George's
Geranio
Hamburger Hamlet
Hard Times Cafe

La Bergerie
la Madeleine
Landini Brothers
Le Bon Cafe
Le Gaulois
Le Refuge
Lite 'n' Fair
Potowmack Landing
R.T.'s
Santa Fe East
Southside 815
Stella's
Taverna Cretekou
Tavola
Tempo
Terrazza
T.G.I. Friday's
Union St. Public Hse.
Warehouse Grill

Arlington/Crystal City/ Ballston/Shirlington

American Cafe
Atami
Atlacatl
Bangkok Gourmet
Bistro Bistro
Bob & Edith's
Cafe Dalat
Cafe Saigon
Cambodian
Carlyle Grand Cafe
Chesapeake Seafood
Crisp & Juicy
Crystal Thai
D'Angelo
Delhi Dhaba
Faccia Luna
Food Factory
Grill, RC, Pent.
Hamburger Hamlet
Hard Times Cafe
Havana Cafe
Hsian Foong
Hunan Number One
Kabul Caravan
Kramerbooks
La Cote d'Or
Lebanese Taverna
Little Viet Garden
Matuba
Nam Viet
Outback Stkhse.
Pasha Cafe
Pho 75
Pines of Italy
Queen Bee
Red Hot & Blue
Rio Grande Cafe
Ruth's Chris
Tachibana
Woo Lae Oak

Burke/Fairfax/Springfield

American Cafe
Anita's
Artie's
Connaught Place
Fern St. Bistro
Generous George's
Houlihan's
Ledo Pizza
Mick's
Mike's Amer. Grill
Outback Stkhse.

Great Falls

Dante
Falls Landing
La Bonne Auberge
L'Auberge Ch. Francois

Leesburg/Manassas/ The Plains/Clifton

Anita's
Fortune
Ledo Pizza
Outback Stkhse.
Red Hot & Blue
T.G.I. Friday's

McLean/Falls Church/ Vienna/Annandale

American Cafe
Anita's
Baron's
Boss Cats
Calif. Pizza Kit.
Clyde's
Da Domenico
Duangrat's
Evans Farm Inn
Generous George's
Haandi
Hunan Lion
Kazan
La Mirabelle
Nizam's
Panjshir
Peking Gourmet
Pho 75
Pilin Thai
Rabieng
Tara Thai
T.G.I. Friday's
That's Amore
Restaurant, RC, Tysons

Orange

Willow Grove Inn

Reston/Herndon/Chantilly

Anita's
Armadilla Grill
Bertucci's
Clyde's
Fortune
Hard Times Cafe
Il Cigno
Outback Stkhse.
Paolo's
Rio Grande Cafe
T.G.I. Friday's
Tortilla Factory

SPECIAL FEATURES AND APPEALS

Breakfast
(All major
hotels and
the following)
Anita's
Bistro Français
Bistro Bravo
Bob & Edith's
Cafe Mozart
Calvert Grille
Cheesecake Factory
Dean & DeLuca Cafe
Florida Ave. Grill
Inn at Glen Echo
Kramerbooks
La Brasserie
La Cote d'Or
La Colline
la Madeleine
Le Bon Cafe
Louisiana Express
Martin's Tavern
Montego Cafe
Nathans
Old Ebbitt Grill
Patisserie Didier
Pho 75
Silver Diner
Starke's BBQ
TooJay's
Warehouse Grill
West End Cafe

Brunch
(*Some good bets)
Aangan
Allegro*
America*
American Cafe
Artie's
Austin Grill/South Austin Grill
Belmont Kitchen
Bilbo Baggins
Bistro Bistro*
Bistro Bravo
Bistro Français
Bistro Le Monde
Bleu Rock Inn
Blue Point Grill
Bombay Bistro
Bombay Club*
Bombay Palace

Cactus Cantina
Cafe Petitto
Cafe BaBaLu
Calvert Grille
Carlyle Grand Cafe*
Chadwicks
Chardonnay*
Chart House*
Cheesecake Factory
China Canteen
Cities
Citronelle*
Clyde's*
Coeur de Lion
Collector, The
Colonnade, The
Connaught Place
D'Angelo
Dean & DeLuca Cafe (M St.)
Delhi Dhaba
Ecco Cafe
Elysium*
Evans Farm Inn
Fedora Cafe
Filomena
Fleetwood's*
Foggy Bottom Cafe
Four Rivers
4 & 20 Blackbirds*
Gabriel*
Gangplank
Garden Cafe*
Georgetown Grill
Georgetown Seafood
Georgia Brown's*
Grill, RC, Pent.*
Grill from Ipanema
Guards
Hamburger Hamlet
Hogate's
Houlihan's
I Matti*
Imperial Hotel*
Inn at Glen Echo
Iron Gate
J. Paul's
Jefferson*
Kinkead's*
Kramerbooks
La Brasserie
La Cote d'Or
Lafayette*
Lauriol Plaza

Coffeehouses & Sweets

(Besides Barista, Border Books, Caffe' Northwest, Ferrara, Politics & Prose, Racheli's, Sirius and Starbucks)
Dean & DeLuca Cafe
Firehook Bakery
Kramerbooks
Le Bon Cafe
Palais du Chocolat
Patisserie Didier

Dancing/Entertainment

(Check days, times and performers for entertainment; D = dancing)
Allegro (harp, piano)
Andalucia (guitar)
Baron's (piano)
Bistro Bistro (jazz)
Bistro 2015 (piano)
Bombay Club (piano)
Cafe Atlantico (D.J.)
Cafe Mozart (piano)
Coeur de Lion (piano)
Colonnade, The (piano)
Coventry Cross (jazz, blues)
D'Angelo (guitar)
Dfouny (bellydancer)
Dixie Grill (bands)
Duangrat's (Thai dance)
Ecco Cafe (jazz)
Evans Farm Inn (piano)
Fedora Cafe (piano)
Fes (bellydancer)
Firehook Bakery (blues, jazz)
Fleetwood's (blues)
Gary's (piano)
Georgetown Grill (jazz)
Georgia Brown's (band)
Grill, RC, Pent. (piano)
Head's (guitar)
Hogate's (jazz)
Imperial Hotel (jazz)
Inn at Glen Echo (jazz)
Kramerbooks (varies)
Lafayette (piano)
La Ferme (piano)
La Mirabelle (piano)
La Tomate (piano)
Le Bon Cafe (guitar)
Lulu's (jazz)
Meskerem (music, trad. dance)
Music City Roadhouse (varies)

Nathans (varies)
Otello (piano)
Paolo's (jazz)
Pasta Place (piano)
Perry's (drag show)
Phillips Flagship (jazz)
Pier 7 (trio, vocalist)
Pines of Italy (piano)
Polly's Cafe (blues)
Prime Rib (piano)
Restaurant, RC, Tysons (jazz)
River Club (D, band)
Sam & Harry's (jazz)
Seasons (jazz)
Sesto Senso (D.J.)
701 (jazz)
State of the Union (D, jazz)
Taverna Cretekou (music)
Terramar (guitar)
Tivoli (piano)
Tuscana West (D.J.)
West End Cafe (guitar)
Willow Grove Inn (vocalist)
Wurzburg-Haus (accordion)

Delivers*/Takeout

(Nearly all Asians, coffee shops, delis, diners & pizzerias deliver or do takeout; here are some best bets; D = delivery, T = takeout)
Allegro (T)
America (T)
American Cafe (D,T)
Armadilla Grill (T)
Atlacatl (T)
Belmont Kitchen (D,T)
Bilbo Baggins (T)
Bistro Bravo (D,T)
Bistro Français (T)
Bistro Le Monde (T)
Blue Point Grill (T)
Cafe Atlantico (T)
Cafe BaBaLu (T)
Cafe Berlin (T)
Cafe Bethesda (T)
Cafe Mozart (D,T)
Capitol City Brew (T)
C.F. Folks (D,T)
Cheesecake Factory (D)
Chicken Place (D,T)
"Ciao baby" (D,T)
Cities (T)
Clyde's (T)
Coeur de Lion (T)

Veneziano (D,T)
Warehouse Grill (T)
Wurzburg-Haus (T)
(*Call to check range and
charges, if any)

Dessert & Ice Cream
(Besides Baskin Robbins,
Ben & Jerry's, Bob's Famous,
Haagen-Dazs, Jeffrey's,
Steve's, Thomas Sweet,
Swensen's, I Can't Believe
It's Yogurt)
Artie's
BICE
Bilbo Baggins
Bistro Bistro
Cheesecake Factory
Citronelle
Clyde's
Dean & DeLuca Cafe
Firehook Bakery
Galileo
Garden Cafe
Inn/Little Wash.
Kinkead's
la Madeleine
L'Auberge Ch. Francois
Mick's
Morrison-Clark Inn
Nora
Obelisk
Pleasant Peasant
701
1789
Ruppers
Seasons
Silver Diner
Southside 815
Stella's
Tivoli
West End Cafe

Dining Alone
(Other than hotels)
Allegro
Coco Loco
Coeur de Lion
Dean & DeLuca Cafe
Jefferson
Kinkead's
Lafayette
Melrose
Patisserie Didier
Provence
Seasons

Fireplaces
(* Check locations)
Aditi
Armadilla Grill
BeDuCi
Bilbo Baggins
Bleu Rock Inn
Chadwicks
Chart House*
Dixie Grill
El Caribe*
Elysium
Evans Farm Inn
Falls Landing
4 & 20 Blackbirds
Gangplank
Geranio
Grill, RC, Pent.
Guards
Houlihan's*
Imperial Hotel
Inn/Little Wash.
Iron Gate
Jefferson
La Chaumiere
La Ferme
la Madeleine
La Mirabelle
L'Auberge Ch. Francois
L'Auberge Provencale
Le Gaulois
Lulu's
Marquis de Rochambeau
Mike's Amer. Grill
Monocle
Old Angler's Inn
Polly's Cafe
Potowmack Landing
Red Sage
Ruth's Chris
Santa Fe East
Sea Catch
1789
Willow Grove Inn

Health/Spa Menus
(Most places cook to order to
meet any dietary request; call
in advance to check; almost
all health food spots, Chinese,
Indian and other ethnics have
health-conscious meals, as
do the following)
Asia Nora
Belmont Kitchen
Bistro 2015

Sheraton/Tysons
  Baron's
State Plaza Hotel
  Garden Cafe
Tabard Inn
  Tabard Inn
Watergate Hotel
  Jean-Louis
  Palladin
Willard Hotel
  Willard Room
Willow Grove Hotel
  Willow Grove Inn

"In" Places

Asia Nora
Austin Grill
BICE
Bistro Français
Busara
Cactus Cantina
Cafe Milano
C.F. Folks
Cheesecake Factory
"Ciao baby"
Cities
Citronelle
City Lights of China
Coco Loco
Coppi's
Cottonwood Cafe
Ecco Cafe
Fleetwood's
Florida Ave. Grill
Galileo
Georgia Brown's
Germaine's
Herb's
Houston's
I Matti
I Ricchi
Jaleo
Jefferson
Jockey Club
La Bergerie
La Brasserie
La Chaumiere
La Colline
Lafayette
L'Auberge Ch. Francois
Le Caprice
Monocle
Morton's of Chicago
Nathans
Nora

Paolo's
Peking Gourmet
Perry's
Pesce
Pizzeria Paradiso
Polly's Cafe
Powerscourt
Prime Rib
Red Sage
Rio Grande Cafe
Rupperts
Sesto Senso
State of the Union
Stella's
Sushi-Ko
Tara Thai
Tom Tom
Tuscana West
Two Quail

Jacket Required

Baron's
Jean-Louis
Jefferson
Jockey Club
L'Auberge Ch. Francois
L'Auberge Provencale
Le Lion d'Or
Marquis de Rochambeau
Melrose
Mr. K's
Palladin
Prime Rib
River Club
1789
Taberna del Alabardero
Willard Room

Late Late – After 12:30

(All hours are AM)
Anita's (24 hrs.)*
America (1)
American Cafe (3)
Bistro Français (4)
Bob & Edith's (24 hrs.)
Cafe Milano (1)
Cafe Petitto (1)
Chadwicks (1)
China Inn (2)
Clyde's (1)*
Ecco Cafe (1)
El Tamarindo (2)
Fleetwood's (1:30)
Full Kee (3)
Generous George's (1)*

Good Fortune (1)
Hard Rock Cafe (1)
Hunan Number One (1:45)
J. Paul's (1)
Kramerbooks (1)
Le Bon Cafe (4)
Marquis de Rochambeau (4)
Martin's Tavern (1)
Meskerem (1)
Montego Cafe (6)
Old Ebbitt Grill (1)
Paolo's (2)
Perry's (1)
Phillips Flagship (1)
Planet Hollywood (1)
River Club (1)
Sequoia (12:45)
Seven Seas (1)
Silver Diner (3)
T.G.I. Friday's (1)*
Tom Tom (1)
Tuscana West (1:30)
Woo Lae Oak (1)
(*Check locations)

Noteworthy Newcomers* (37)
Arucola**
Asia Nora
B. Smith's**
Boss Cats
Caffe Pazzo**
Cafe BaBaLu
"Ciao baby" Cucina
Coco Loco
Coventry Cross
Crescent City
D'Angelo
Eat First
Fes
Fleetwood's
Gabriel
Gerard's Place
Hibiscus Cafe
Il Radicchio
Kinkead's
la Madeleine
Les Halles
Little Fountain Cafe
Miss Saigon
Music City Roadhouse
Oval Room
Palladin
Pesce
Planet Hollywood

Provence
R.T.'s Seafood Kitchen**
Rupperts
Sesto Senso
Southside 815
Stella's
Tara Thai
Tom Tom
Tuscana West
(*Open under a year at *Survey* time; **not open yet, looks promising;)

Noteworthy Closings (18)
Blue Bayou
City Cafe
Dominique's
Dona Flor
Duke Zeibert's
El Patio
Fish Wings & Tings
Gaslight
House of Hunan
Jonah's
Kabul West
La Plaza
Le Steak
Mimmetta's
Szechuan
Unkai
Yannick's
Zia Mia

Offbeat
Armadilla Grill
Bob & Edith's
Boss Cats
C.F. Folks
Cities
Coco Loco
Dixie Grill
Fes
Florida Ave. Grill
Generous George's
Grill from Ipanema
Hard Rock Cafe
Hibiscus Cafe
Jaleo
Kramerbooks
Lauriol Plaza
Little Fountain Cafe
Montego Cafe
Music City Roadhouse
Perry's
Pho 75

Polly's Cafe
Red Sage
Red Sea
Rupperts
Skewers
State of the Union
Tabard Inn
Tom Tom
Tony Cheng's

Outdoor Dining

(G = Garden; P = Patio;
R = Rooftop; S = Sidewalk;
T = Terrace; W = Waterside;
*check locations)
America (S)
American Cafe (P)*
Anita's (P)
Atlacatl (G,P,T)
Bacchus (P)
Bangkok Gourmet (P)
Bangkok Orchid (G)
Belmont Kitchen (P)
BICE (P)
Bistro Bistro (S)
Bistro Bravo (S)
Bleu Rock Inn (T,W)
Blue Point Grill (P)
Bombay Club (P)
Boss Cats (P)
Busara (G)
Cactus Cantina (P)
Cafe Atlantico (S)
Cafe BaBaLu (R)
Cafe Berlin (T)
Cafe Bethesda (S)
Cafe Milano (P)
Cafe Saigon (S)
Cantina Romana (G,T)
Carlyle Grand Cafe (P,S)
C.F. Folks (P)
Chardonnay (T)
Chart House (P)
Chesapeake Seafood (P)
Clyde's (P,W)*
Coco Loco (P)
Colonnade, The (P)
Cottonwood Cafe (P)
Crisp & Juicy (S)*
D'Angelo (P)
Dante (P)
Dean & DeLuca Cafe (P)
Donatello (S)
Donna Adele (P)
Duangrat's (S)

Evans Farm Inn (G)
Faccia Luna (P,S)
Falls Landing (P)
Fleetwood's (P,W)
Galileo (G)
Garden Cafe (P)
Gangplank (P,W)
Generous George's (P)*
Geppetto (S)
Gerard's Place (S)
Gulf Coast Kitchen (P)
Hamburger Hamlet (P,W)*
Hibiscus Cafe (P)
Hisago (P,W)
Hogate's (P,W)
Houlihan's (P)*
Il Cigno (P,W)
Il Forno (P)
Imperial Hotel (G)
Inn at Glen Echo (P)
Inn/Little Wash. (G)
Iron Gate (G)
Ivy's Place (S)
Jaimalito's (P,W)
Kinkead's (P)
Kramerbooks (S)
La Brasserie (P)
La Colline (P)
La Cote d'Or (P)
La Ferme (T)
La Fourchette (P)
la Madeleine (P)
La Miche (S)
La Tomate (P)
L'Auberge Ch. Francois (G)
L'Auberge Provencale (P)
Lauriol Plaza (P)
Lebanese Taverna (S)
Le Bon Cafe (P)
Le Caprice (S)
Le Rivage (T,W)
Les Halles (P)
Little Fountain Cafe (G)
Little Viet Garden (P)
Louisiana Express (P)
Lulu's (P)
Martin's Tavern (S)
Melrose (T)
Mick's (P)*
Miss Saigon (P)
Montego Cafe (T)
Montgomery's Grille (T)
Morrison-Clark Inn (T)
Mrs. Simpson's (P)
Music City Roadhouse (P,W)

Outstanding Views

Parking

(L = Parking Lot;
V = Valet Parking;
CP = Validated Parking;
$ = Discount Parking;
* = Suburban locations;
** = check locations)

113

La Bergerie (CP)
La Bonne Auberge (L)
La Brasserie (L,V)
La Chaumiere (CP)
La Colline (CP) (eve)
La Cote d'Or (L)
Lafayette (CP,V,$)
La Ferme (L)
La Fourchette (L,$)
la Madeleine (L)
La Miche (V,eve $)
La Mirabelle (L)
Landini Brothers (CP)
La Tomate (CP)
L'Auberge Ch. Francois (L)
L'Auberge Provencale (L)
Lauriol Plaza (L)
Lebanese Taverna (L)
Le Bon Cafe (V)**
Le Caprice (V,$)
Ledo Pizza (L)
Le Lion d'Or (CP,L) (eve)
Le Mistral (V)
Le Rivage (V)
Les Halles (V,$)
Le Vieux Logis (L,V)
Listrani's (L)
Lite 'n' Fair (L)**
Little Viet Garden (L)
Luigino (L,$)
Lulu's (CP)
Madeo (L,$)
Maison Blanche (L,V)
Marquis de Rochambeau (L,$)
Martin's Tavern (CP)
Matuba (L)**
Melrose (V)
Metro Center Grille (L,$)
Mick's (L)**
Mike's Amer. Grill (L)
Miss Saigon (L,$)
Monocle (V)
Montgomery's Grille (L,CP)
Morrison-Clark Inn (L,V)
Morton's of Chicago (V) (eve)
Mr. K's (V) (eve)
Music City Roadhouse (L)
Mykonos (V) (eve)
Nam's (L)
Nam's of Bethesda (L)
Nam Viet (L)
New Heights (V) (eve)
Nicholas (CP)
Nizam's (L)
Notte Luna (V) (eve $)

O'Brien's (L)
O'Donnell's (L)
Occidental Grill (CP,L,V)
Old Angler's Inn (L)
Old Ebbitt Grill (V)
Outback Stkhse. (L)
Oval Room (V) (eve)
Palladin (L,V)
Palm, The (V) (eve)
Panjshir (L)
Paolo's (L)
Parioli (V)
Pasha Cafe (L)
Pasta Place (L,$)
Pasta Plus (L)
Patisserie Didier (L,$)
Peasant Rest. (CP,V)
Peking Gourmet (L)
Persepolis (L) (eve)
Phillips Flagship (L,$)
Phillips Grill (L,V,$)
Pho 75 (L)
Pier 7 (CP)
Pilin Thai (L)
Pines of Italy (L)
Planet Hollywood (V,$) (eve)
Pleasant Peasant (L,V,CP)
Potowmack Landing (L)
Powerscourt (V,$)
Prime Rib (V) (eve)
Primi Piatti (V)
Provence (V) (eve)
Queen Bee (CP)
Rabieng (L)
Red Hot & Blue (L)**
Red Sage (CP,$)
Renato (L)
Restaurant, RC, Tysons (CP,L,V)
Rio Grande Cafe (L)
River Club (V)
Rupperts (L)
Ruth's Chris (V) (eve)
Saigon Gourmet (L)
Saigonnais (L,$)
Sakura Palace (L)
Sam & Harry's (V) (eve)
Santa Fe East (CP,$)
Sea Catch (L)
Seasons (CP,V)
Sequoia (CP,$)
Sesto Senso (V,$)
701 (V)
Seven Seas (L)
1789 (V)
Sfuzzi (CP)

Silver Diner (L)
Southside 815 (L)
Starke's BBQ (L)
Stella's (CP)
Sunny Garden (L)
Sushi-Ko (V,$) (eve)
Taberna del Alabardero (V) (eve)
Tachibana (L)
Taipei/Tokyo Cafe (L)
Tara Thai (L)
Taste of Saigon (L)
Tempo (L)
Terramar (V,$) (eve)
T.G.I. Friday's (CP,L)**
Thai Kingdom (CP) (eve)
That's Amore (L)
Tiberio (V) (eve)
Tivoli (CP) (eve)
Tomato Palace (L)
Tony & Joe's (L,$)
TooJay's (L)
Tortilla Factory (L)
Tragara (V)
Trattu (V)
Trumpets (L,$)
Tuscana West (V)
Veneziano (CP)
Vidalia (V) (eve)
Vincenzo (V) (eve)
Volare (V,$) (eve)
West End Cafe (V)
Willard Room (CP,V)
Willow Grove Inn (L)
Woo Lae Oak (L)
Wurzburg-Haus (L)

Parties & Private Rooms

(Any nightclub or restaurant
charges less at off hours;
* indicates private rooms
available; best of many)
America*
Armadilla Grill
Asia Nora
Bacchus*
Belmont Kitchen*
BICE*
Bilbo Baggins*
Bistro 2015*
Bombay Palace*
Cafe Milano*
Cafe Pierre*
Calvert Grille*
Cantina Romana*
Celadon*

"Ciao baby"*
Cities*
Citronelle*
Clyde's*
Colonnade, The*
D'Angelo*
Dante*
Dixie Grill*
Donna Adele*
Duangrat's*
Ecco Cafe*
Evans Farm Inn*
Falls Landing*
Fleetwood's*
Fortune*
4 & 20 Blackbirds*
Galileo*
Gangplank*
Gary's*
Generous George's*
Geranio*
Grill, RC, Pent.*
Guards*
Hard Times Cafe*
Head's*
Hisago*
Hunan Chinatown*
Hunan Lion*
Hunan Manor*
Ichiban*
Il Cigno*
I Matti
Imperial Hotel*
Inn at Glen Echo*
Inn/Little Wash.*
Iron Gate*
Jaimalito's*
Jean-Louis*
Jefferson*
J. Paul's*
Kawasaki*
Kazan*
Kinkead's*
La Bonne Auberge*
La Brasserie*
La Chaumiere*
La Colline*
Lafayette*
La Ferme*
La Fourchette*
la Madeleine*
La Miche*
Landini Brothers*
La Tomate*
L'Auberge Provencale*

Le Caprice*
Le Gaulois*
Le Lion d'Or*
Le Mistral*
Les Halles*
Lulu's*
Madeo*
Maison Blanche*
Martin's Tavern*
Mick's*
Mixtec*
Monocle*
Morrison-Clark Inn*
Morton's of Chicago*
Mr. K's*
Music City Roadhouse*
Mykonos*
Nicholas*
Nizam's*
Nora*
Occidental Grill*
Odeon Cafe*
Old Angler's Inn*
Old Ebbitt Grill*
Old Glory BBQ*
Palladin*
Paolo's*
Parioli*
Pasta Place*
Peasant Rest.*
Peking Gourmet*
Perry's*
Persepolis*
Phillips Flagship*
Pier 7*
Potowmack Landing*
Powerscourt*
Primi Piatti*
Provence
Red Hot & Blue*
Red Sage*
Restaurant, RC, Tysons*
River Club*
Ruth's Chris*
Sam & Harry's*
Sea Catch*
Seasons*
Sequoia*
Sesto Senso*
701*
1789*
Sfuzzi*
State of the Union*
Steamers*
Straits of Malaya*

Tabard Inn*
Taberna del Alabardero*
Terrazza*
Thai Place*
That's Amore*
Tia Queta*
Tivoli*
Tony Cheng's*
Tortilla Factory
Tragara*
Two Quail*
Union St. Public Hse.*
Vincenzo*
Warehouse Grill*
West End Cafe*
Willow Grove Inn*
Woo Lae Oak*

People-Watching
America
Artie's
Belmont Kitchen
BICE
Bistro Français
Busara
Cactus Cantina
Cafe Atlantico
Cafe BaBaLu
Cafe Milano
Carlyle Grand Cafe
Cheesecake Factory
"Ciao baby"
Cities
Coco Loco
Cottonwood Cafe
Dixie Grill
Filomena
Fleetwood's
Florida Ave. Grill
Gabriel
Galileo
Georgia Brown's
Germaine's
Guards
Herb's
Hibiscus Cafe
Houston's
I Matti
I Ricchi
Jaleo
J. Paul's
Jaimalito's
Kinkead's
Kramerbooks
L'Auberge Ch. Francois

La Brasserie
La Colline
Lafayette
La Fourchette
Lauriol Plaza
Les Halles
Maison Blanche
Monocle
Nathans
Nora
Notte Luna
Occidental Grill
Old Ebbitt Grill
Old Glory BBQ
Oval Room
Paolo's
Perry's
Pier 7
Prime Rib
Rio Grande Cafe
Ruppers
701
Seasons
Sfuzzi
Tabard Inn
Tiberio
Tom Tom
Tuscana West
Willard Room

Power Scenes
BICE
Bombay Club
C.F. Folks
Citronelle
Coco Loco
Coeur de Lion
Colonnade, The
Galileo
Gary's
Germaine's
Georgia Brown's
Head's
I Ricchi
Inn/Little Wash.
Jean-Louis
Jefferson
Jockey Club
La Bergerie
La Brasserie
La Colline
Lafayette
Landini Brothers
L'Auberge Ch. Francois
Le Caprice

Le Lion d'Or
Le Mistral
Maison Blanche
Monocle
Morton's of Chicago
Mr. K's
Occidental Grill
Oval Room
Palm, The
Powerscourt
Prime Rib
Primi Piatti
Provence
Ruppers
Sam & Harry's
Seasons
Taberna del Alabardero
Willard Room

Pre-Theater Menus
(Call to check prices,
days and times)
Artie's
Bamiyan
BICE
Bilbo Baggins
Bistro Bistro
Bistro Français
Bleu Rock Inn
Bombay Club
Cafe Bethesda
Carlyle Grand Cafe
Celadon
"Ciao baby"
Citronelle
Clyde's
D'Angelo
Donatello
Elysium
Filomena
Gangplank
Garden Cafe
Grill from Ipanema
Houlihan's
Ivy's Place
Jean-Louis
La Fourchette
Lavandou
Le Refuge
Le Rivage
Lite 'n' Fair
Luigino
Madeo
Marquis de Rochambeau
Melrose

118

Saigonnais
Sala Thai
Santa Fe East
Sarinah Satay House
Sea Catch*
Sequoia*
Seven Seas
Silver Diner
Skewers
Southside 815
Starke's BBQ
Star of Siam
Steamers
Sunny Garden
Taipei/Tokyo Cafe
Tara Thai
Taste of Saigon
Taverna Cretekou
Tempo
T.G.I. Friday's
Thai Flavor
Thai Kingdom
Thai Place
Thai Taste
Tia Queta
Tomato Palace*
Tony & Joe's*
TooJay's
Tortilla Coast
Tortilla Factory
Tung Bor
Union St. Public Hse.
Veneziano
Warehouse Grill
West End Cafe*
Woo Lae Oak
Wurzburg-Haus

Senior Appeal

Anita's
Cafe Bethesda
Chadwicks
Chart House
Cheesecake Factory
Clyde's
Crisfield
D'Angelo
Evans Farm Inn
Falls Landing
Gangplank
Inn at Glen Echo
Jockey Club
L'Auberge Ch. Francois
La Ferme
O'Donnell's

Pines of Italy
Pines of Rome
Potowmack Landing
1789
Silver Diner
Willard Room
Wurzburg-Haus

Singles Scenes

America
Artie's
Austin Grill
Bistro Bistro
Bistro Français
Busara
Cafe Atlantico
Cafe BaBaLu
Cafe Milano
Capitol City Brew
Carlyle Grand Cafe
Chadwicks
Chart House
"Ciao baby"
Cities
Clyde's
Cottonwood Cafe
Dixie Grill
Ecco Cafe
Faccia Luna
Filomena
Fleetwood's
Gangplank
Georgetown Grill
Grill from Ipanema
Guards
Herb's
Hogate's
Houston's
Jaleo
Jaimalito's
Jockey Club
J. Paul's
Kramerbooks
La Colline
Lauriol Plaza
Martin's Tavern
Mike's Amer. Grill
Montego Cafe
Montgomery's Grille
Nathans
Notte Luna
Occidental Grill

Odeon Cafe
Old Angler's Inn
Old Ebbitt Grill
Old Glory BBQ
Paolo's
Pasta Place
Perry's
Pier 7
Polly's Cafe
Prime Rib
Rio Grande Cafe
River Club
R.T.'s
Sam & Harry's
Sequoia
Sesto Senso
701
Sfuzzi
T.G.I. Friday's
Tom Tom
Tony & Joe's
Tortilla Coast
Tuscana West
Union St. Public Hse.
Warehouse Grill
West End Cafe

Sleepers
(Good to excellent food,
but little known)
Cantina Romana
Celadon
China Canteen
Connaught Place
Dfouny
Garden Cafe
Ginza's
Il Cigno
Imperial Hotel
Kabul Caravan
Kawasaki
Lite 'n' Fair
Little Fountain Cafe
Miss Saigon
Nam's
Pasha Cafe
Pilin Thai
Rabieng
Sunny Garden
Tempo
Thai Flavor
Tomato Palace
Willow Grove Inn

Teflons
(Gets lots of business,
despite so-so food, i.e.
they have other attractions
that prevent criticism from
sticking)
Capitol City Brew
Chadwicks
Hard Rock Cafe
Houlihan's
Planet Hollywood
Phillips Flagship
Silver Diner
T.G.I. Friday's

Smoking Prohibited
(May be permissible at
bar or outdoors)
Asia Nora
Bangkok Gourmet
Bertucci's
Blue Point Grill
Cafe Bethesda
Cafe Dalat
Cafe Pierre
Calif. Pizza Kit.
Carlyle Grand Cafe
C.F. Folks
Crystal Thai
D'Angelo
Dante
Eat First
4 & 20 Blackbirds
Firehook Bakery
Frog & the Redneck
Hinode
Houlihan's
Il Forno
Imperial Hotel
Inn/Little Wash.
Iron Gate
Ivy's Place
Jean-Michel
L'Auberge Provencale
Lebanese Taverna
Le Bon Cafe
Ledo Pizza
Le Vieux Logis
Listrani's
Matuba
Morrison-Clark Inn
Mrs. Simpson's
Nam's
Nora
Obelisk

Old Ebbitt Grill
Palais du Chocolat
Parioli
Pasta Place
Pilin Thai
Pizzeria Paradiso
Renato
Stella's
Taipei/Tokyo Cafe
Tara Thai
Terramar
TooJay's
Vietnam Georgetown
Vincenzo
Volare

Sunday Dining

(B = brunch; L = lunch;
D = dinner; plus all hotels
and most Chinese; * check
location; ** some good bets)
Aangan (B,D)
America (B,L,D)
American Cafe (B,L,D)*
Aditi (L,D)
Alekos (L,D)
Allegro (B,L,D)
Andalucia (D)**
Anita's (L,D)
Appetizer Plus (D)
Armadilla Grill (D)*
Artie's (B,D)*
Atami (L,D)
Atlacatl (L,D)
Austin Grill (B,L,D)**
Bamiyan (L,D)*
Bangkok Gourmet (D)
Bangkok Orchid (L,D)
Belmont Kitchen (B,D)
Bertucci's (L,D)
BICE (D)
Bilbo Baggins (B,D)
Bistro Bistro (B,D)
Bistro Bravo (B,L)
Bistro Français (B,L,D)
Bleu Rock Inn (B,D)
Bistro 2015 (L,D)
Blue Point Grill (B,D)
Bob & Edith's (L,D)
Bombay Bistro (B,D)
Bombay Club (B,D)**
Bombay Palace (B,D)
Boss Cats (L,D)
Burma (D)
Busara (L,D)

Cactus Cantina (B,D)**
Cafe Atlantico (D)
Cafe BaBaLu (B,L,D)
Cafe Berlin (D)
Cafe Dalat (L,D)
Cafe Milano (L,D)
Cafe Mozart (L,D)
Cafe Petitto (B,L,D)
Cafe Pierre (L,D)
Cafe Saigon (L,D)
Cajun Bangkok (D)
Calif. Pizza Kit. (L,D)
Calvert Grille (B,L,D)
Cantina Romana (D)
Capitol City Brew (L,D)
Carlyle Grand Cafe (B,L,D)
Carnegie Deli (L,D)
Celadon (D)**
Chadwicks (B,L,D)
Chardonnay (B,D)
Chart House (B,D)
Cheesecake Factory (B,L,D)
Chesapeake Seafood (D)
Chicken Place (L,D)
China Canteen (B,D)
China Chef (L,D)
China Inn (L,D)
"Ciao baby" (D)
Cities (B,D)**
Citronelle (B,D)**
City Lights of China (L,D)
Clyde's (B,D)**
Coco Loco (D)**
Coeur de Lion (B,D)**
Collector, The (B,D)
Colonnade, The (B)
Connaught Place (B,D)
Coppi's (D)**
Cottonwood Cafe (D)
Crisfield (D)
Crisp & Juicy (L,D)
Crystal Thai (L,D)
D'Angelo (B,D)**
Dante (D)
Dean & DeLuca Cafe (B,L,D)*
Delhi Dhaba (B,D)
Dfouny (L,D)
Donna Adele (D)
Donatello (D)
Duangrat's (L,D)
Dusit (L,D)
East Wind (D)
Eat First (L,D)
Ecco Cafe (B,L,D)
El Caribe (L,D)

Prime Rib
Primi Piatti
Provence
Red Sage
Restaurant, RC, Tysons
Sam & Harry's
Seasons
1789
Taberna del Alabardero
Terrazza
Tiberio
Tivoli
Tragara
Vincenzo
Willard Room

Wheelchair Access

(Check for bathroom access;
almost all hotels plus the
following; best bets;
*check locations)
Aangan
Alekos
America
American Cafe
Andalucia
Anita's
Appetizer Plus
Armadilla Grill
Artie's
Bacchus
Bertucci's
BICE
Bilbo Baggins
Bistro Bistro
Bistro Bravo
Bistro Le Monde
Blue Point Grill
Bob & Edith's
Bombay Club
Bombay Palace
Boss Cats
Cafe Milano
Cafe Mozart
Cafe Saigon
Calif. Pizza Kit.
Calvert Grille
Cambodian
Capitol City Brew
Carlyle Grand Cafe
C.F. Folks
Chadwicks*
Chart House
Cheesecake Factory
Chicken Place

China Inn
"Ciao baby" Cucina
Citronelle
Clyde's
Collector, The
Colonnade, The
Connaught Place
Coppi's
Cottonwood Cafe
Crisp & Juicy
Crystal Thai
Da Domenico
Dante
Dean & DeLuca Cafe
Delhi Dhaba
Dfouny
Donna Adele
Dusit
East Wind
Eat First
Ecco Cafe
El Caribe
Enriqueta's
Evans Farm Inn
Faccia Luna*
Fedora Cafe
Fern St. Bistro
Fes
Firehook Bakery
Fleetwood's
Food Factory
Foong Lin
Fortune
Full Kee
Gabriel
Gaby's
Galileo
Gangplank
Gary's
Generous George's
Georgia Brown's
Geppetto*
Good Fortune
Grill, RC, Pent.
Grill from Ipanema
Gulf Coast Kitchen
Haandi
Hamburger Hamlet
Hard Rock Cafe
Hard Times Cafe*
Herb's
Hibiscus Cafe
Hinode
Hogate's
Houlihan's

Terrazza
T.G.I. Friday's (most)
Thai Kingdom
Thai Place
That's Amore
Tia Queta
Tomato Palace
Tony & Joe's
TooJay's
Tortilla Coast
Tortilla Factory
Tragara
Tung Bor
Volare
West End Cafe
Willard Room
Wurzburg-Haus

Wine & Beer Only

Anita's
Appetizer Plus
Bombay Bistro
Cafe Bethesda
Calif. Pizza Kit.
Cambodian
Chesapeake Seafood
China Canteen
Crisfield
Delhi Darbar
Delhi Dhaba
Eat First
Generous George's
Hard Times Cafe
Hibiscus Cafe
Hinode
Il Forno
Il Pizzico
Il Radicchio
Ivy's Place
la Madeleine
Ledo Pizza
Listrani's
Lite 'n' Fair
Louisiana Express
Matuba
Mixtec
Nam's
Pasta Plus
Pesce
Pines of Rome
Pizzeria Paradiso
Queen Bee
Renato
Silver Diner
Starke's BBQ

Tako Grill
Tomato Palace
Wurzburg-Haus

Winning Wine Lists

Artie's
BICE
Cafe Mozart
Chardonnay
Citronelle
Colonnade, The
Galileo
Gerard's Place
Germaine's
I Ricci
Inn/Little Wash.
Jean-Louis
Jefferson
Jockey Club
L'Auberge Ch. Francois
La Brasserie
La Colline
Lafayette
Le Lion d'Or
Maison Blanche
Morrison-Clark Inn
Nicholas
Obelisk
Palladin
Prime Rib
Provence
Sam & Harry's
1789
Taberna del Alabardero
Tiberio
Tivoli
Tragara
Vincenzo

Worth a Trip

MARYLAND
Chestertown
    Imperial Hotel
Potomac
    Old Angler's Inn
St. Michael's
    Inn at Perry Cabin
VIRGINIA
Flint Hill
    4 & 20 Blackbirds
Great Falls
    Dante
    L'Auberge Ch. Francois
Orange
    Willow Grove Inn

BALTIMORE

Baltimore's Most Popular Restaurants

Each of our reviewers has been asked to name his or her five favorite restaurants. The 30 spots most frequently named, in order of their popularity, are:

1. Milton Inn
2. Tio Pepe
3. The Prime Rib
4. Linwood's
5. Hampton's
6. Brass Elephant
7. Polo Grill
8. Outback Steakhouse
9. M. Gettier
10. Chart House
11. Red Hot & Blue
12. Citronelle
13. Ruth's Chris Steak House
14. Due
15. Rudys' 2900
16. Northwoods/A
17. Marconi's
18. Tabrizi's
19. Peerce's Plantation
20. Haussner's
21. Paolo's
22. Kings Contrivance
23. Treaty of Paris/A
24. Tersiguel's
25. Pierpoint
26. Pavilion at the Walters
27. Boccaccio
28. Akbar
29. T.G.I. Friday's
30. Spike & Charlie's

It's obvious that most of the restaurants on the above list are among the most expensive, but Baltimore diners love a bargain. Were popularity calibrated to price, we suspect that a number of other restaurants would join the above ranks. Thus, we have listed over 70 "Best Buys" on pages 141 and 142.

A = Annapolis.

Top Ratings*

Top 30 Food Ranking

27	Hampton's		Pierpoint
26	Milton Inn		La Piccolo Roma/A
	Prime Rib		Tersiguel's
25	M. Gettier	22	Ruth's Chris
	Linwood's		Jeannier's
	Tio Pepe		Helmand
	Citronelle		Puffin's
24	Polo Grill		Bombay Grill
	Rudys' 2900		Brass Elephant
	Inn at Perry Cabin		Kawasaki
	Northwoods/A		Da Mimmo
	Stone Mill Bakery		Treaty of Paris/A
23	Tabrizi's		Pavilion at the Walters
	Boccaccio		Marconi's
	Due	21	Cantler's Riverside/A

Top Spots by Cuisine

Top American (Contemporary)
27 Hampton's
26 Milton Inn
25 Linwood's
   Citronelle
24 Polo Grill

Top Breakfast†
24 Stone Mill Bakery
21 Cafe Normandie/A
   Donna's
20 Morning Edition
16 Woman's Indust. Exch.

Top Brunch
27 Hampton's
24 Polo Grill
23 Pierpoint
22 Treaty of Paris/A
   Pavilion at the Walters

Top Business Lunch
25 Linwood's
24 Polo Grill
23 Boccaccio
   Due
   La Piccolo Roma/A

Top Chinese
20 Hoang's
   Tony Cheng's
19 Szechuan Best
18 Bamboo Hse.
17 Uncle Lee's

Top Continental
25 Tio Pepe
24 Rudys' 2900
   Northwoods/A
22 Marconi's
21 Peerce's Plantation

Top Crab Houses
21 Cantler's Riverside/A
20 Obrycki's
17 Gunning's
   Bo Brooks

Top Family Dining
21 Cantler's Riverside/A
   Red Hot & Blue
20 Chart House
19 Sabatino's
18 Haussner's

* Excluding restaurants with low voting.
† Other than hotels.
A = Annapolis.

Top French
25 M. Gettier
23 Tersiguel's
22 Jeannier's
21 Cafe Normandie/A
20 Orchid

Top Health Food
23 Tabrizi's
22 Puffin's
18 Dalesio's
   Harvey's
17 Stixx Cafe

Top Hotel Dining
27 Hampton's/
   Harbor Court Hotel
25 Citronelle/Latham Hotel
24 Polo Grill/
   Inn at the Colonnade
22 Treaty of Paris/
   Maryland Inn
18 Windows/Stouffer's

Top Italian
23 Boccaccio
   Due
   La Piccolo Roma/A
22 Da Mimmo
21 Germano's

Top Japanese
25 Kawasaki
20 Shogun
   Hoang's
18 Sushi Cafe
   CoChin

Top Newcomers/Rated
25 M. Gettier
   Citronelle
24 Stone Mill Bakery
23 Due
21 Donna's

Top Newcomers/Unrated
   Boathouse
   Donna's at BMA
   Loco Hombre
   PaperMoon
   Piccolo's

Top Pizza
20 Al Pacino Cafe
19 Mama Lucia/A
17 BOP
16 Ledo
14 Milano's

Top Seafood
23 Pierpoint
21 Cantler's Riverside/A
20 Chart House
19 Carrol's Creek/A
   Gibby's

Top Steakhouses
26 Prime Rib
22 Ruth's Chris
20 McCafferty's
   Outback Steakhse.
18 Hersh's Orchard

Top Worth a Drive
26 Milton Inn/
   Sparks
24 Rudys' 2900/
   Finksburg
   Inn at Perry Cabin/
   St. Michael's
21 Peerce's Plantation/
   Phoenix
20 Josef's/
   Fallston

Top 30 Decor Ranking

28 Hampton's
26 Inn at Perry Cabin
    Milton Inn
24 Citronelle
    Linwood's
    Prime Rib
23 Polo Grill
    Berry & Elliot's
    Treaty of Paris/A
    Brass Elephant
    Pavilion at the Walters
22 Haussner's
    Peerce's Plantation
    Lista's
    Windows

21 Boccaccio
    Due
    Kings Contrivance
    Tersiguel's
    Northwoods/A
    Chart House
20 Rudys' 2900
    Tio Pepe
    McCafferty's
    Taverna Athena
    Carrols Creek/A
    Harry Browne's/A
    Paolo's
    M. Gettier
    Ruth's Chris

Top Outdoor

Bay Cafe
Cantler's Riverside/A
Carrols Creek/A
Chart House
Lista's
McGarvey's/A

Middleton Tavern/A
Nickel City
Paolo's
Peerce's Plantation
Pier 500
Taverna Athena

Top Rooms

Brass Elephant
Citronelle
Donna's at BMA
Hampton's
Haussner's
Linwood's

Lista's
Milton Inn (Hearth Room)
Pavilion at the Walters
Polo Grill
Prime Rib
Treaty of Paris/A

Top Views

Bamboo House
Bay Cafe
Berry & Elliot's
Carrols Creek
Chart House
Citronelle

Hampton's
Peerce's Plantation
Pier 500
Taverna Athena
Waterside
Windows

Top 30 Service Ranking

26 Hampton's
25 Milton Inn
Prime Rib
24 Citronelle
Linwood's
M. Gettier
Inn at Perry Cabin
23 Rudys' 2900
Northwoods/A
22 Polo Grill
Due
Marconi's
Treaty of Paris/A
21 Tersiguel's
Helmand

Boccaccio
Ruth's Chris
Tio Pepe
La Piccolo Roma/A
Tabrizi's
Peerce's Plantation
Da Mimmo
20 Pavilion at the Walters
McCafferty's
Pierpoint
Windows
Jeannier's
Brass Elephant
Kings Contrivance
Taverna Athena

Best Buys

Top 50 Bangs For The Buck

This list reflects the best dining values in our *Survey*. It is produced by dividing the cost of a meal into the combined ratings for food, decor and service.

1. Stone Mill Bakery
2. Woman's Indust. Exch.
3. Bertucci's
4. Silver Diner
5. Attman's Deli
6. Al Pacino Cafe
7. Baugher's
8. Red Hot & Blue
9. Helmand
10. Donna's
11. Ledo Pizza
12. Marmaduke's Pub/A
13. Bertha's
14. Louie's Bookstore Cafe
15. Akbar
16. Bare Bones
17. Mick's
18. Taverna Athena
19. Ikaros
20. Bombay Grill
21. McGarvey's/A
22. John Steven Ltd.
23. Lista's
24. T.G.I. Friday's
25. Mama Lucia/A
26. Great Amer. Melting Pot
27. Bohager's
28. Uncle Lee's
29. Alonso's
30. Sisson's
31. Outback Steakhse.
32. Kawasaki
33. Cantler's Riverside/A
34. American Cafe
35. Henry & Jeff's
36. Red Star
37. Bamboo House
38. Windows
39. Hoang's
40. Pavilion at the Walters
41. Harvey's
42. Paolo's
43. Sfuzzi
44. Milano's
45. Morgan Millard
46. Burke's Cafe
47. Cafe Normandie/A
48. Tony Cheng's
49. Haussner's
50. Puffin's

A = Annapolis.

Additional Good Values
(A bit more expensive, but worth every penny)

Amicci's

Angelina's

Banjara

BOP

Cafe Hon

Cafe Manet

Cafe Troia

Chart House/A

Chiapparelli's

Clyde's/A

CoChin

Corinthian

Cover to Cover Cafe

Friendly Farms

Gibby's

Gypsy's Cafe

Hampton's (brunch)

Henninger's

Josef's

Little Campus Inn/A

Loco Hombre

Martick's

Mencken's

Middleton Tavern/A

Morning Edition

Mt. Washington Tavern

New No Da Ji

Nickel City

O'Brien's/A

Orchard Market

Palermo's Grill

PaperMoon

Raphael's

Regi's

Sam's Waterfront Cafe

Shogun

Southwest Passage

Strapazza

Szechuan Best

Thai

Thai Landing

Vanguard Cafe

Water St. Exchange

Weber's on Boston

Alphabetical
Directory
of Restaurants

Akbar S   20 | 14 | 19 | $17
823 N. Charles St. (bet. Madison & Read Sts.), 410-539-0944
3541 Brenbrook Dr. (Liberty Rd.), Randallstown,
410-655-1600
■ Besides serving cheap "dependable Indian food", this "mysterious" Mount Vernon Mogul has "its own identity" as a "local folks' place"; its Randallstown sibling provides the same spicy curries and "customer attention", but in "warehouse"-like space.

Alonso's ◐ S   17 | 7 | 13 | $13
415 W. Cold Spring Ln. (bet. Charles St. & Roland Ave.),
410-235-3433
◩ A perfect specimen of an endangered species – a scruffy, dark, "traditional Baltimore neighborhood bar"; this legend has good beer, a "bartender who hates the Redskins" and the superburger "of your dreams" – "we're talking a mammoth" 14 oz. or more.

Al Pacino Cafe ◐ S   20 | 9 | 14 | $13
(aka Egyptian Pizza)
609 S. Broadway (bet. Fleet & Aliceanna Sts.),
410-327-0005 ◐
900 Cathedral St. (Read St.), 410-962-8859
Belvedere Sq., 542 E. Belvedere Ave. (York Rd.), 410-323-7060
■ "Inventive" pizzas like tandoori chicken with peach chutney and authentic Middle Eastern specialties may "deserve an Oscar", but few would give these no-frills pizza-makers beauty or sociability prizes; still, they don't charge blockbuster prices, and you can always take the food home.

Ambassador Dining Room S   – | – | – | M
Ambassador Apts., 3811 Canterbury Rd. (39th St.),
410-467-4799
A "hidden treat", with lovely alfresco dining, this once-staid dining room (near Johns Hopkins) isn't like that anymore; energetic owners have updated its American classics menu and attracted a younger clientele; happily, the feeling of dining in an Old Baltimore mansion remains.

American Cafe S   15 | 14 | 15 | $16
Harborplace, Light St. Pavilion, 410-962-8800
Owings Mills Mall, 10300 Mill Run Circle (off I-795),
Owings Mills, 410-363-3400
10400 Little Patuxent Pkwy. (next to Columbia Mall),
Columbia, 410-740-7200
2 W. Pennsylvania Ave. (bet. York Rd. & Washington Ave.),
Towson, 410-321-4800
See Washington, DC, Alphabetical Directory.

Amicci's [S] ▽ | 20 | 14 | 19 | $18
231 S. High St. (bet. Stiles & Fawn Sts.), 410-528-1096
■ "Very small", "rushed", "casual" and cheap; this engaging storefront takes a fresh approach to Littly Italy tradition, piling up more red-sauced pasta and seafood than the "table can hold", with "blues music" and a good buzz as background; "go early to get a table."

Angelina's [S] | 18 | 9 | 15 | $19
7135 Harford Rd. (Rosalie Ave.), 410-444-5545
■ Only in Baltimore would you find a "white-bread" Irish bar specializing in Italian food that gets awards for the "best crab cake in the world"; most reviewers "don't order anything else", though the North Baltimore "neighborhood" atmosphere and Gaelic music are also "worth coming for."

Attman's Delicatessen [S] | 19 | 6 | 12 | $11
1019 E. Lombard St. (bet. Lloyd & Watson Sts.), 410-563-2666
◪ Where locals take visitors to see "a real Jewish deli" and get a real corned beef sandwich "stacked a mile high"; the kibbitzing countermen are as salty as ever, however, the Lombard Street premises and neighborhood have "seen better days" (to put it kindly); P.S. they cater.

Baltimore Brewing Company [S] | 11 | 16 | 14 | $17
104 Albemarle St. (bet. Lombard & Pratt Sts.), 410-837-5000
◪ Like a beer garden "in Germany", the courtyard of this brewpub near the Inner Harbor is a "great place to hang out" over "home brew"; though "they try hard", the "snack" food is merely ballast for the "great beer."

Bamboo House [S] | 18 | 19 | 18 | $20
Harborplace, Pratt St. Pavilion, 410-625-1191
Yorktowne Plaza Shopping Ctr., 26 Cranbrook Rd. (York Rd.), Cockeysville, 410-666-9550

Joey Chiu's Greenspring Inn
10801 Falls Rd. (Greenspring Valley Rd.), Lutherville, 410-823-1125
■ Now that these popular "pretty places" serve sushi, along with "dependable (multiregional) Chinese", you can combine grazing with Inner Harbor views; despite the different names, all three sites offer a "lovely ambiance" for business or meeting friends; their focus on "quality" and "care in the details, shows."

Bangkok Place [S] ▽ | 21 | 14 | 17 | $17
5230 York Rd. (bet. Cold Spring Ln. & Woodbourne Ave.), 410-433-0040
■ "A nice Thai pad for nice pad Thai", this unpretentious North Baltimore Thai uses "fresh ingredients" in "very clean" tasting-menu standards; if that's "too tame", order one of the specials and tell the kitchen to turn up the heat.

Banjara S
▽ 21 | 18 | 18 | $14

*1017 S. Charles St. (bet. Hamburg St. & Cross St. Market),
410-962-1554*

■ This Federal Hill Indian "neighborhood place" gives ethnic dining a good name; its "authentic" food is well prepared and politely served in "pleasant" candlelit surroundings, and its lunch buffet is a best deal.

Bare Bones S
20 | 14 | 17 | $17

*St. John's Plaza, 9150 Baltimore Nat'l. Pike (one light west of Rte. 29), Ellicott City, 410-461-0770
617 S. Frederick Ave. (½ mile north of Shady Grove Rd.), Gaithersburg, 301-948-4344*

■ What "devoted carnivores" want is lotsa "good ribs" with minimal decor, since decor just gets in the way of eating "sloppy"; these "family-style rib houses" do the job for a "low price" with "great greasy onion rings" to really "blow your diet"; a bit more consistency and faster service wouldn't hurt.

Baugher's S ⌿
14 | 6 | 15 | $11

*289 W. Main St. Ext. (Rtes. 31 & 32), Westminster,
410-848-7413*

■ The "small town atmosphere" pervading this Carroll County farmstand/restaurant is fostered by waitresses and "prices from another era" and a menu of "old-fashioned food like moms made" generations back; it's a favored family outing for people from all walks of life, with homemade-tasting pies, "great ice cream", and fresh fruit to take home.

Bay Cafe ◗ S
12 | 14 | 12 | $18

Tindeco Wharf, 2809 Boston St., 410-522-3377

☑ In lovely weather, sailors and singles set their course for this dockside watering hole where they capture the "right table" for a "great view" and "shrimp salad sandwich" but "you can feel like an outsider" if you're not into those scenes, and you may not find solace in the "average" bar nibbles and slowly served seafood.

Benny's Restaurant & Jazz Club S
– | – | – | M

2701 N. Charles St. (27th St.), 410-366-7779

In Mount Vernon, "wonderful jazz" in an upbeat supper-club setting to the accompaniment of Benny Gordon's Cajun cooking; it sounds great, tastes down-home and couldn't be more affordable – entrees on the à la carte menu peak at $12.95; dinner and live jazz, Thursday–Saturday nights only.

BERRY & ELLIOT'S ◑ Ⓢ 　　20｜23｜19｜$28

Hyatt Regency Baltimore, 300 Light St. (bet. Pratt & Conway Sts.), 410-528-1234

▪ Almost every table in this rooftop room affords sublime harbor views and happily the "beautifully presented" Contemporary American food helps maintain your high if you choose carefully; focus on "delicious" seafood and steak.

Bertha's Ⓢ 　　19｜16｜16｜$16

734 S. Broadway (Lancaster St.), 410-327-5795

▪ For many, Bertha's "spells" mussels, but there's a "lot more" to this raunchy, "dark woody" Fells Point institution than fits on a bumper sticker – such as its "repertoire" of draft beer, Scottish tea with "lemon scones", shepherd's pie and seafood, "great jazz" and "real local color"; it all adds up to "eccentric fun."

Bertucci's 　　18｜16｜16｜$15

8130 Corporate Place (Honeygo Blvd.), 410-931-0900
Snowden Sq., 9081 Snowden River Pkwy. (Robert Fulton Dr.), Columbia, 410-312-4800
Owings Mills Mall, 10300 Mill Run Circle (off I-795), Owings Mills, 410-356-5515
2207 Forest Dr. (Rte. 2 & Riva Rd.), Annapolis, 410-266-5800
See Washington, DC, Alphabetical Directory.

Boathouse Crab Deck 　　–｜–｜–｜M
& Raw Bar, The Ⓢ

515 S. Eden St. (Eastern Ave.), 410-675-3808, 1-800-366-CRAB

It looks like trend-setters Jim Mikula and Tim Douglas (Weber's, Bohager's) have dreamed up another winner – a 'dirty-to-the-elbows' crab-and-seafood shack for twenty/thirtysomethings, next door to Bohager's; it's open-air and ought to be a smashing success; May–October only.

Bo Brooks Crab House Ⓢ 　　17｜9｜14｜$20

5415 Belair Rd. (Frankford Ave.), 410-488-8144

◪ There may be better, cheaper, less crowded, more colorful crab houses in Baltimore, but few have this "barnlike" spot's "reputation" for having high-quality crabs, in and "out of season"; although there's a variety of seafood on the menu, "you're doing yourself a disservice if you don't order (steamed hard) crabs."

BOCCACCIO Ⓢ 　　23｜21｜21｜$32

925 Eastern Ave. (bet. Exeter & High Sts.), 410-234-1322

▪ At the high-end of Little Italy dining in terms of prices and patina (and, some add, "pretensions"), many consider its "sophisticated" Northern Italian food "unmatched" – if occasionally "disappointing"; chef-owner Giovanni Rigato is clearly "capable of good things in the kitchen", though "not so good on reservations."

Bohager's Bar and Grill S   13 | 15 | 13 | $14
515 S. Eden St. (Fleet St.), 410-563-7220
■ What really makes this Downtown place is the bar, the music, a cool happy hour and being "outdoors" on a "summer night"; the grilled pizza and pork BBQ can be good, but "bring a megaphone" if you want to converse.

Bombay Grill S   22 | 18 | 19 | $20
2 E. Madison St. (N. Charles St.), 410-837-2973

Bombay Peacock Grill S
10005 Old Columbia Rd. (Eden Brook Rd.), Columbia, 410-381-7111
■ The "gentle atmosphere" and studied graciousness of this Mount Vernon "classic Indian" harmonizes with its "delicious", variably seasoned food; thus it can be enjoyed by fire-eaters as well as "those squeamish about spicy" dishes; if you live or work near Columbia, try its equally "serene" and "superior" sibling.

"BOP" Brick Oven Pizza ● S   ▽ 17 | 7 | 11 | $11
800 S. Broadway (Lancaster St.), 410-563-1600
■ We're told the new owners of this Fells Point pizza shop aren't changing the crisp-crusted "brick-oven pizzas" (why fix what ain't broke?), they're just adding some decor and seats along with pastas and dessert; as for adjusting its "alternative rock attitude", let's hope not.

BRASS ELEPHANT, THE S   22 | 23 | 20 | $31
924 N. Charles St. (bet. Read & Eager Sts.), 410-547-8480
■ Few Baltimore restaurants can match the Edwardian elegance of this wonderful, recently refurbished Mt. Vernon residence, but some find its "very good" Northern Italian food and "attentive" service "inconsistent"; now, it looks like the "new chef's" contemporary touch is giving it a boost; either the three-course $7.50 lunch or $15.95 pre-theater is a cheap way to check it out.

Burke's Cafe ● S   15 | 11 | 14 | $15
36 Light St. (Lombard St.), 410-752-4189
☑ "Timeworn, but still useful" for courthouse lawyers and late-night revelers, this "scruffy" corner tavern may still serve (loosely speaking) decent burgers, but saying that "Burke's tastes like Bawlmer" is defaming Charm City.

Cacao Lane S   17 | 18 | 17 | $24
8066 Main St. (Tiber Alley), Ellicott City, 410-461-1378
☑ You couldn't ask for more "inviting", "romantic" rusticity than this "charming old stone building" in historic Ellicott City; however, its Continental and light fare and service are so "hit or miss" that they frustrate diners—in sum, once you're there, "there's not a lot there."

Caesar's Den S | 21 | 16 | 19 | $25 |
223 S. High St. (Stiles St.), 410-547-0820

■ Many believe that this standby embodies the "best of Little Italy"—meaning that it's a "dependable, comfortable" place run by "really nice people" where "everything is made to order" and tastes "good"; a few don't see it on the cutting edge, but if you care about the basics, it's a gem.

Cafe Hon ⌨ | ▽ 16 | 10 | 17 | $10 |
1009 W. 36th St. (bet. Roland Ave. & Falls Rd.), 410-243-1230

◩ "You'll go again" and again to this endearingly "amateurish" Hampden cafe for its "honest-to-goodness", "short-order" home cooking, plus "great salads, mashed potatoes", memorable meat loaf and forget-the-calorie desserts; it's straight out of an Anne Tyler novel, causing some to wonder "is this for real?"

Cafe Manet | ▽ 18 | 12 | 14 | $16 |
1020 S. Charles St. (Cross St.), 410-837-7006

■ Little bigger than a food stall in the nearby Cross Street Market, this chipper, Euro-style cafe is short on service and space, but long on affordable "French-Continental dishes" and wines; chances are you'll leave "very contented."

Cafe Normandie S | 21 | 19 | 19 | $23 |
185 Main St. (bet. Church Circle & Conduit St.), Annapolis, 410-263-3382

■ The ambiance and cooking of a "French country inn" and a Gallic regard for "good value" make this bistro one of the most popular restaurants in historic Annapolis; it's "very pleasant" for lunch and has "excellent crêpes", but a few sticklers question its French credentials.

Cafe Troia | 20 | 17 | 18 | $28 |
Penthouse Condominiums, 28 W. Allegheny Ave. (Washington Ave.), Towson, 410-337-0133

◩ Known for its "truly authentic" Regional Italian food and dressed-down demeanor, this celebrated Towson restaurant is still "trying to absorb its growth"; while regrets about its popularity are not uncommon, most surveyors say it's still "nice for casual dining" with dishes not found elsewhere.

California Pizza Kitchen S | – | – | – | I |
Annapolis Mall, 22 Annapolis Mall (Jennifer Rd.), Annapolis, 410-573-2060
See Washington, DC, Alphabetical Directory.

Cantler's Riverside Inn S
21 | 14 | 17 | $19
*458 Forest Beach Rd. (on Mills Creek), Annapolis,
410-757-1311*
■ On a hot July night, "nothing beats" sitting "on the water"
at this back-road crabshack near Annapolis — or finding
"a cocktail waitress in the parking lot" (yes, it's that busy);
go early and "wear your grubbies" for smashing hard shells,
and if you don't enjoy deconstructionist dining there's
plenty of other fresh seafood and soft shells as well.

Carrols Creek Cafe S
19 | 20 | 18 | $24
*410 Severn Ave. (East Port Bridge), Annapolis,
410-263-8102, in Baltimore call 410-269-1406*
■ A popular choice for Annapolis "waterscape" dining on
"first-rate" Contemporary seafood in a loosened-tie
milieu; however, the "glorious bay views" are "possible"
only if you get the right table and the staff sometimes
"seems incapable of 'getting it right'"; "best" at brunch.

CHART HOUSE S
20 | 21 | 19 | $26
*300 Second St. (Severn Ave.), Annapolis, 410-268-7166, in
Baltimore call 410-269-6992
Pier 4, 601 E. Pratt St., 410-539-6616*
See Washington, DC, Alphabetical Directory.

Chiapparelli's S
18 | 14 | 18 | $22
237 S. High St. (Fawn St.), 410-837-0309
■ Over the past 50 years, this "Little Italy institution" has
become a tradition for family visits thanks to its secret-
formula "best salad in the universe", its "predictable"
pastas, seafood and veal, "mom"-like waitresses and
"old-fashioned" rooms — as Yogi Berra would say, it'll
"survive (another 50 years) due to longevity."

CITRONELLE S
25 | 24 | 24 | $42
*The Latham Hotel, 612 Cathedral St. (Monument St.),
410-837-3150*
■ "Tout Baltimore" celebrates the marriage of its most
"spectacular" view, overlooking the Monument, with Michel
Richard's "California nouvelle cuisine"; a meal at this
offshoot of his renowned LA-based Citrus is "innovative",
"fanciful" and usually unrushed — but what's a "wow" if
"Richard is there" can be "mediocre without" him, and
not everyone appreciates its wicker-and-white "LA" look.

Clyde's ◑ S
17 | 19 | 18 | $20
10221 Wincopin Circle (Rte. 175), Columbia, 410-730-2828
See Washington, DC, Alphabetical Directory.

CoChin S   ▽ 18 | 18 | 19 | $18

800 N. Charles St. (Madison St.), 410-332-0332
■ Step down from Mt. Vernon Square into a "cool, modern" enclave with "caring" staff and "interesting" pan-Asian cuisine: "you can order authentic Vietnamese" ("generous with garlic and hot peppers"), more subdued Chinese-French-influenced dishes or sushi, all at wallet-friendly prices; the $6.95 Vietnamese lunch buffet is a good intro.

Corinthian S   ▽ 24 | 24 | 23 | $27

Loews Annapolis Hotel, 126 West St. (Lafayette St.), Annapolis, 410-263-1299
■ In Annapolis, for "fine dining in a relaxed atmosphere", there is no "surer bet" than this Contemporary American dining room; its muted setting is a business lunch dream, but the real deal comes at night – for a $22.95 prix fixe, you get candlelight cosseting and, *inter alia*, the "best steak in the city."

Cover to Cover Bookstore & Cafe S   ▽ 19 | 13 | 17 | $16

Owen Brown Village Ctr., 7284 Cradlerock Way, Columbia, 410-381-9200
■ This art-filled Columbia bookstore cafe successfully combines reading, "light" eating and looking; it's a "nice place to "relax" with friends over high tea or a contemporary meal and some wicked sweets; reactions to its "new age" atmosphere and service may depend on one's age.

Crab Shanty S   16 | 16 | 15 | $20

3410 Plumtree Dr. (Rte. 40 W.), Ellicott City, 410-465-9660
◪ The carnival atmosphere and Eastern shore cooking ("heavy, fatty") remind some of Ocean City's high-volume, family seafood "barns", but this "Route 40 restaurant" (halfway between Baltimore and DC) strikes some as strictly for "locals" with "Amex" cards.

CrossRoads S   ▽ 15 | 14 | 13 | $24

Cross Keys Inn, 5100 Falls Rd. (Cold Spring Ln.), 410-532-6900
■ With "few restaurants in the (Uptown) area" and plenty of pass-by traffic, this spare, "trendy"-looking hotel dining room may be a useful address for your Rolodex; we hear its American steak-and-seafood menu and service are "much improved lately" and it's adept with "large groups."

Dalesio's of Little Italy S   18 | 16 | 16 | $25

829 Eastern Ave. (Albemarle St.), 410-539-1965
◪ "Out of the ordinary for Little Italy", this intimate (if "cramped") townhouse prides itself on using local produce and pure ingredients in its Northern Italian recipes and in its tasty spa cuisine; though it goes "off and on", its fans rank it among the "best."

	F	D	S	C

Da Mimmo ◐ S
22 | 17 | 21 | $34

217 S. High St. (Stiles St.), 410-727-6876

▨ Tuxedo-class dining amidst unabashed glitz; this "very dark", "small-and-busy" Italian does such "transcendent" things with its hefty veal chop and seafood specials and is run by such "gracious" hosts that most diners forgive its "condescending" waiters and high prices; however, others dub it "da Gypo."

Donna's at the BMA S
– | – | – | M

Baltimore Museum of Art, Art Museum Dr. (N. Charles St.), 410-467-3600

Early this fall, Donna Crivello opened this "lovely" Eclectic-American restaurant, outdoor cafe and coffeehouse overlooking the BMA sculpture garden; given her prior success at producing up-to-the-minute fare in a "scenic" environment (Donna's Restaurant), one can now look forward to visiting the BMA not just for viewing.

Donna's Restaurant S
21 | 17 | 18 | $18

800 N. Charles St. (Madison St.), 410-539-8051

Donna's Coffee Bar S
2 W. Madison St. (N. Charles St.), 410-385-0180
22 W. Allegheny Ave. (bet. Washington Ave. & York Rd.), Towson, 410-828-6655

■ This "appealing" young American bistro brings big-city "sophistication" Downtown with "lots of pasta and organic greens", artisan pizzas and au courant grills in an understated setting that's almost as "cool" as the help; next door, and in Towson, her coffee bars do cappuccino and "fabulous breads", "roasted veggies" and dessert to such loud applause that you "must lip-read to converse."

DUE S
23 | 21 | 22 | $29

25 Crossroads Dr. (McDonough Rd.), Owings Mills, 410-356-4147

■ "Coming on strong" as "one of the area's most creative" restaurants, Linwood Dame's "rustic" trattoria inspires Owings Mills diners to want to "eat their way through the menu" of ever-changing, Tuscan-inspired pizza, pasta and contadina (farm food) aided by "servers who know the answers to your questions"; most look beyond any "kinks" to see its "promise."

Eager House S
▽ 18 | 18 | 16 | $26

(aka Murphy's Eager House)
15 W. Eager St. (Charles St.), 410-783-4268

▨ Old-timers go "sentimental" over the "classic" (dark and clubby) decor, "piano player" and "sometimes just perfect" Old Baltimore–New American food at this Downtown dress-up reincarnation; but "inept service" and a "'what's my line' menu" cause some to say "too little, too late."

Fiori [S] 17 18 17 $25

100 Painters Mill Rd. (Dolfield Rd.), Owings Mills, 410-363-3131

◪ "Slightly dated" refers to this Continental-Italian's food, atmosphere and clientele, not its imposing 18th-century Owings Mills habitation; though capable of providing "a fine evening out" (if you "order the specials" or light fare in the wine cellar bar), it can also be "disappointing."

Fisherman's Wharf [S] 19 14 18 $24

Dulaney Valley Shopping Ctr., 826 Dulaney Valley Rd. (Fairmont Ave.), Towson, 410-337-2909

◪ The portions of top-quality seafood at this "functional" fish house "could sink a ship" (but not your budget) and its customers can't keep track of the "many ways" it's cooked; the problem is that "close-to-home" convenience comes with a "commercial" environment and "suburban sprawl."

Foster's Wine Bar & Restaurant ☽ [S] ▽ 18 16 17 $27

606 S. Broadway (bet. Fleet & Aliceanna Sts.), 410-558-3600

■ A good place to soak up "Fells Point atmosphere" at a lazy "Saturday lunch", this attractive seafood restaurant has a new management and kitchen (not reflected in ratings) that is now featuring regional seafood and affordable wines; drop by for Tuesday night tastings.

Freds [S] 18 15 18 $23

2348 Solomons Island Rd. (1 block from Parole Shopping Ctr.), Annapolis, 410-224-2386, in Baltimore call 410-841-6890, 1-800-773-7347

◪ It's not just tourists en route to the shore who routinely stop for crab cakes: this '50s-era restaurant is also a "locals' mainstay"; while the rest of the seafood, steak and Southern Italian menu may not be worth a drive, it's "sorta fun" to relax in the old-fashioned, red plush rooms and chat with the "blue-hair" waitresses.

Friendly Farms [S] 14 10 16 $17

17434 Foreston Rd. (Mt. Carmel Rd.), Upperco, 410-239-7400

◪ When the kids want a "ride in the country" and mom doesn't want to cook, this Upperco destination "fills the family inexpensively"; look for "home-cooked" comfort food and family-style service in a "kitchen"-like setting; crab cakes and duck-watching are highlights.

Germano's Trattoria [S] 21 18 20 $27

300 S. High St. (Fawn St.), 410-752-4515

■ To learn about the Tuscan food of this Little Italy "mom-and-pop shop" simply "ask Germano what he recommends"; surveyors not only enjoy the "good food and value", but also the brick walls brightened by art deco posters; only a few traditionalists wish he'd stop "tinkering with the menu."

Gibby's S
　　　　　　　　　　　　　　19 | 14 | 17 | $20
22 W. Padonia Rd. (Broad St.), Cockeysville, 410-560-0703
■ Timonium fish house that serves "terrific crab entrees" and "the biggest, best shrimp ever"; of course, when you cook "every creature that's ever been in a Jacques Cousteau special", there are bound to be some "misses", and apart from hosting a "good" neighborhood bar, the ambiance is zilch.

Great American
Melting Pot, The ◗ S (aka Gampy's)
　　　　　　　　　　　　　　15 | 13 | 17 | $16
904 N. Charles St. (Read St.), 410-837-9797
◪ The "best thing happening after 2 AM" (on weekends), this is where everyone who craves "greasy food late at night" chows down on everything from French toast to fondue; one thing about this "fun" Charles Street "dive", it's not wimpy – the Eclectic-American food and service are either "super-super good or super bad."

Gunning's Crab House S
　　　　　　　　　　　　　　17 | 9 | 16 | $20
3901 S. Hanover St. (Jeffrey St.), 410-354-0085
7304 Parkway Dr. (Dorsey Rd., Rte. 176), Hanover,
410-712-9404
■ There are now two Gunning's: the old one, a vintage Brooklyn crab house famous for crabs, "fried green pepper rings" and salty service, and the new Gunning's, off Dorsey Road, opened by the Gunning family after they sold the old one; don't worry if you're confused – both feature the good old recipes and call-you-"hon" waitresses.

Gypsy's Cafe ◗ S
　　　　　　　　　　　▽ 19 | 16 | 16 | $17
1103 Hollins St. (S. Arlington Ave.), 410-625-9310
■ An eclectic bistro for Baltimore's "Generation X-slacker-chic" set, this inviting jumble near Hollins Market is a neat place to settle in the garden in summer or by the "wood-burning fireplace" and take the "chill off a snowy day" with whatever the cooks feel like cooking; Baltimore's "grunge-rock" types eat here, but don't let that keep you away.

HAMPTON'S S
　　　　　　　　　　　　　　27 | 28 | 26 | $48
Harbor Court Hotel, 550 Light St. (bet. Conway & Lee Sts.),
410-234-0550
■ The "most beautiful (and expensive) room in town" was made for celebrating life's "special occasions" and "impressing guests"; it's one of those "exceptional" urbane places where first-rate modern American food (and new regional specials), fine wine and elegant service come together to leave you feeling "pampered" and relaxed; it's such a "superior" operation that a post-*Survey* chef change shouldn't matter.

Harry Browne's S　　　　20 │ 20 │ 19 │ $26 │
66 State Circle (bet. Maryland Ave. & E St.), Annapolis,
410-263-4332, in Baltimore call 410-269-5124
■ This classy dining room "on the Circle" is a "State House
favorite" that illustrates the maxim that the "best restaurant
is the one that knows you best"; yet its strengths go beyond
its strategic location and ability to take "good care" of
friends, to include "enjoyable" Continental food, a
"hideaway" ambiance and a casual backyard cafe.

Harryman House S　　　　19 │ 18 │ 19 │ $24 │
340 Main St. (1 1/4 miles north of Franklin Blvd.),
Reisterstown, 410-833-8850
■ A colonial-era destination that has more than its fair
share of rustic "charm"; it also has pretty good American
food that works well for a "quiet dinner" or an antiquing
lunch; the pubby bar, with nearly 80 beers, is where the
"Greenspring Valley crowd" meet their "friends."

Harvey's S　　　　18 │ 17 │ 18 │ $20 │
Greenspring Station, 2360 W. Joppa Rd. (Falls Rd.),
Lutherville, 410-296-9526
■ This "upscale" suburbanite has a California-style menu
that goes from "spa cuisine" to chicken Szechuan, and has
enough indoor and outdoor space to accommodate "the
grandchildren" as well as the business diners who don't
want to sit near them; when crowded, it sometimes sputters.

Haussner's　　　　18 │ 22 │ 19 │ $24 │
3242 Eastern Ave. (Clinton St.), 410-327-8365
■ No one should miss the "Baltimore experience" of
dining at this venerable "museum" of art and kitsch where
"AARP" help serves reliably good German and Old
Maryland cooking; for the thousands who dine here each
year, "the party's the thing", and though a few say the
"place is starting to droop" ("like its nudes"), it's "a trip."

Helmand, The S　　　　22 │ 18 │ 21 │ $20 │
806 N. Charles St. (bet. Read & Madison Sts.), 410-752-0311
■ Not only did this admirable Mt. Vernon ethnic show
Baltimore that "there's more to Afghan than knitted
blankets", it proved that a low-priced "exotic" can be
"just wonderful" for entertaining clients; it combines
"subtle, delicious" food with a "pretty" room and "warm",
"get-you-to-the-symphony-on-time" service.

Henninger's Tavern　　　　▽ 23 │ 19 │ 22 │ $24 │
1812 Bank St. (bet. Ann & Wolfe Sts.), 410-342-2172
■ A quintessential Fells Point Eclectic pub that seems to
specialize in "warm fuzzy feelings" until you taste its
"excellent" food and don't-skip desserts; being "small and
cozy", no reserving makes it "tough on weekends."

Henry and Jeff's ◑ S   16 | 9 | 12 | $14
1220 N. Charles St. (bet. Biddle & Preston Sts.), 410-727-3322
■ This Belvedere deli is a "good place to go if you don't know what you want" since something on its breakfast/sandwich/Tex-Mex/BBQ-and-grill bill of fare is bound to appeal; it's also a popular place to go before and after almost anything, but it's "not the place to propose."

Hersh's Orchard Inn S   18 | 17 | 18 | $30
1528 E. Joppa Rd. (½ mile west of Loch Raven Blvd.), Towson, 410-823-0384
◪ Unless a "regular", you may not "understand" this old-line, suburban steak and seafooder's "attraction": a clubby ambiance, "large portions" and schmoozing with "nice guy" Hersh; it leaves others shrugging "20 years of wet salad", "I don't care what famous people ate here before."

Hoang's Seafood Grill & Sushi Bar S   20 | 15 | 18 | $20
1619 Sulgrave Ave. (Kelly Ave.), 410-466-1000
◪ Offering four Asian cuisines – Chinese, Thai, Vietnamese and Japanese sushi – as well as grilled seafood, and with barely enough space for a few tables, it's not surprising that this simple Mt. Washington cafe's "talented kitchen", "lovely owner" and "nice staff" sometime get overwhelmed.

Ikaros S   19 | 14 | 19 | $18
4805 Eastern Ave. (bet. Oldham & Ponca Sts.), 410-633-3750
◪ Few restaurants pile on more food for less money than this Greektown hero – and few match its "doggie bag generosity" with so much warmth and friendliness; for best results "go with the staff's recommendations", but dissenters' comments suggest that the food may have flown too close to the sun and had a serious fall.

Il Giardino S   ▽ 18 | 16 | 18 | $24
Golden Triangle Shopping Ctr., 8809 Baltimore Nat'l. Pike (Rte. 29), Ellicott City, 410-461-1122
■ Howard County "steps up from the 'Olive Tree'" to authentic Northern Italian dining in this "surprising" shopping center location; "not your mom's pasta and red sauce", it serves rich "cream sauces" and delicate veal in a gardenlike setting; still some find it "disappointing."

Imperial Hotel Restaurant   ▽ 25 | 24 | 21 | $39
The Imperial Hotel, 208 High St. (Cross St.), Chestertown, 410-778-5000
■ A "lovely Chestertown stop" when touring the Eastern shore, its adventurous American food, "charming" Victorian setting and attentive staff work together to create a very "special" experience; plan your next getaway to include one of its "unsurpassable" wine dinners.

INN AT PERRY CABIN, THE 🇸   24 | 26 | 24 | $47
The Inn at Perry Cabin, 308 Watkins Ln. (Talbot St.),
St. Michaels, 410-745-2200
◼ At this Eastern shore "fantasyland", guests wallow in
faux English manor elegance, are fed "fascinating"
Continental-Eclectic food (contemporary and classical)
and are "pampered" by "experts"; some ask if all that
costly "chintz" and cosseting get a little "cloying", but
most people "can't get there enough."

Jasper's 🇸   11 | 14 | 12 | $17
Commercentre, 1777 Reisterstown Rd. (Hooks Ln.),
410-486-1400
1651 Rte. 3 N. (Rte. 450), Crofton, 301-261-3505, DC,
410-721-0041, Annapolis ◗
Greenway Shopping Ctr., 7401 Greenbelt Rd.
(Balt. Wash. Pkwy.), Greenbelt, 301-441-8030 ◗
◪ Those surveyors who don't trash these "fungible fern
bars" as strictly "eat-to-live" dining find them a "great
value" for families; an exception to their "sit-down fast-
food" image is the Reisterstown site, with a "power lunch."

Jeannier's   22 | 17 | 20 | $28
Broadview Apts., 105 W. 39th St. (Charles St.), 410-889-3303
◼ "Le vrai Baltimore", a "little frumpy", but awfully "reliable"
with "nice French" ("not fancy shmancy") food and "old
shoe" comfort; this "top-of-the-line" apartment-house
dining room is less than 10 years old, but it feels like "the
'50s", especially its early-bird $15.95 prix fixe.

John Steven Ltd. ◗🇸   18 | 15 | 15 | $17
1800 Thames St. (Ann St.), 410-327-5561
◼ This Fells Point blue-collar "classic" keeps updating
itself without losing the raucous, "neighborly" appeal of
its barroom and "wonderful patio"; its modern American
kitchen pleases foodies, yet it has kept its "amazing crab
cakes", incredible beers and hang-loose attitude.

Josef's Country Inn 🇸   ▽ 20 | 17 | 20 | $23
2410 Pleasantville Rd. (Rte. 152), Fallston, 410-877-7800
◼ Trek to this "cozy" Black Forest transplant in Harford
County when you're in the mood for hearty sauerbraten
and heavy gemütlichkeit; by "eating in the bar" you escape
the weekend crowds but lose "candlelight" and kitsch.

Kawasaki   22 | 17 | 19 | $21
413 N. Charles St. (Franklin St.), 410-659-7600
◼ While sushi hasn't replaced crab cakes as this town's
signature dish, it's very in vogue — which makes this
Downtown traditionalist's "best Japanese" rating worthy
of respect; not only is it prized for its "great sit-on-the-floor
sushi", cooked entrees like teriyaki are "enjoyable" too.

Kings Contrivance [S] 20 | 21 | 20 | $31

10150 Shaker Dr. (bet. Rts. 29 & 32), Columbia, 410-995-0500

◪ While this turn-of-the-century "country house" is no longer in the country, it's probably the best "fancy" place around; its Continental fare is often used to seal a deal, or as an agreeable prelude to "Merriweather" concerts, but critics find the food and furbishing "dated", strictly "for Mother's Day"; P.S. avoid weekend nights.

La Piccola Roma [S] 23 | 19 | 21 | $28

200 Main St. (bet. Church Circle & Conduit St.), Annapolis, 410-268-7898

■ Credit the success of this smart-looking Northern Italian to the "professional", warm, "personal supervision" of its owners, Mary and Gino Giolitti, the "younger generation of a Roman restaurant family"; the pasta and risotto taste so "like Italy", they have "single-handedly increased the sophistication of Annapolis dining 100 percent."

Ledo Pizza [S] ⊄ 16 | 7 | 14 | $12

405 N. Center St. (Cranberry St.), Westminster, 410-857-3500
Park Plaza, 552 E. Ritchie Hwy. (Baltimore-Annapolis Blvd.), Severna Park, 410-544-3344
Greenspring Tower, 1020-40 W. 41st St. (Falls Rd.), 410-243-4222
Snowden Ctr., 6955 Oakland Mills Rd. (Snowden River Pkwy.), Columbia, 410-381-5550
11321 York Rd. (Shawan Rd.), Hunt Valley, 410-785-5336

◪ You needn't have grown up in College Park to "acquire a taste" for these suburban pizza parlors' "strangely addicting" pie-crusted, sweet-sauced, "greasy" pizza squares; their "club basement" settings, cheery help and cheap prices appeal to kids of all ages; however, a fair number "hate this style pizza."

LINWOOD'S [S] 25 | 24 | 24 | $35

25 Crossroads Dr. (McDonough Rd.), 410-356-3030

■ In Owings Mills, this handsome, mahogany-and-black Contemporary American is where Baltimorians show off for "people from New York and San Francisco"; its food is "delicious", "light" and full of "surprises", while its ambiance combines "family and sophistication"; but it wouldn't be 'Bal'mer' without a curmudgeon: "if I wanted my string beans artistically arranged, I'd hang them on the wall."

Lista's [S] 16 | 22 | 17 | $19

Brown's Wharf, 1637 Thames St. (Bond St.), 410-327-0040

◪ The "best things" about this "Mexicali fiesta" on the Fells Point waterfront are its imaginative use of wharf space, mega-margaritas, entertaining musicians, outdoor seating and "unmatched view"; but the "cheery" staff stumbles and the Tex-Mex fare is pretty "lame."

Little Campus Inn   ▽ 13 | 10 | 15 | $17

63 Maryland Ave. (bet. State Circle & Prince George St.),
Annapolis, 410-263-9250

■ "What you see is what you get" at this "plain, hometown" American, and what you get is "lots of" wholesome eats for not much money and an "easygoing staff" who "have been there forever"; half a block from the Annapolis State House, it's where those pols water their grass roots.

Loco Hombre S   – | – | – | I

413 W. Coldspring Ln. (Charles St.), 410-889-2233

There's nothing loco about this Classic Catering Group (Polo Grill and Pavilion at the Walters) Tex-Mex quality concept; it's equipped with everything from a hokey "legend" to some downright hearty eating, but most impressive is its classy fresh look; get there early, there's no reserving.

Louie's Bookstore Cafe ● S   17 | 17 | 13 | $15

518 N. Charles St. (bet. Franklin & Centre Sts.), 410-962-1224

☑ "Populated by conforming nonconformists" and with "endearingly ditzy" help, this "artsy" Mt. Vernon bookstore/ cafe with "ambitious casual food", live music and "nice prices" works for dessert, "brunch and eavesdropping"; you can read *War and Peace* without being bothered by a waiter.

Mama Lucia S ⌿   19 | 13 | 15 | $16

Annapolis Plaza, 150H Jennifer Rd. (Rte. 450), Annapolis,
410-266-1666

☑ In Annapolis, a surprising number of satisfying, eat-at-home Italian meals originate at this on-the-way-from-work stop; as for eat-in, that's strictly "self-serve" and seat yourself, but the food is "tasty", "cooked to order" and moderately priced.

Manor Tavern S   18 | 18 | 18 | $25

15819 Old York Rd. (Manor Rd.), Monkton, 410-771-8155

☑ For some city-dwellers, this horse-country hostelry means a "long drive for a great lunch"; for others, it offers "little that's good" in the way of Continentalized-American food and service; locals prefer "informal eating" in the rustic barroom over the formal dining rooms where you "go with your wife's folks."

Marconi's   22 | 15 | 22 | $26

106 W. Saratoga St. (bet. Park Ave. & Cathedral St.),
410-727-9522

■ This legendary townhouse "hasn't changed since grandfather ate there"; its Old Maryland food is still "great", as in chopped salad, lobster Cardinale, creamed spinach and a definitive hot fudge sundae, while the "impeccable service" and time-warp prices are happy reminders of a bygone era; no dinner past 8 PM (9 PM weekends).

Marmaduke's Pub S   18 | 18 | 19 | $18

301 Severn Ave. (3rd St.), Annapolis, 410-268-1656, in Baltimore call 410-269-5420

◪ "If one sails" out of Annapolis, one "après" at this "clubby" mahogany-and-brick saloon; and, while its "international rep" probably isn't based on the beer, burgers, salads or tuna steak sandwich, they go well with salty stories; the upstairs cabaret pulls "too many tourists" to please the "sailing set."

Martick's   19 | 12 | 14 | $25

214 W. Mulberry St. (bet. Park Ave. & Howard St.), 410-752-5155

◪ "You'll either love it or hate it", but this tumbledown old East Baltimore speakeasy "can't be described"; for openers, there's no sign, light or doorknob (look for the "bell above the door"), and the vaguely French food and service is as eccentric as the "70-year-old hippie" who runs the joint seemingly as a hobby.

Matsuri   – | – | – | M

1105 S. Charles St. (Cross St.), 410-752-8561

Patience is rewarded at this engaging, blond-wood-and-tile Federal Hill Japanese; it's long on talent – everything from sushi to robata grills and unusual noodle dishes are carefully prepared and artfully presented – but short on staff and space.

McCafferty's S   20 | 20 | 20 | $29

Catalyst Sq., 1501 Sulgrave Ave. (Newbury St.), 410-664-2200

◪ Up front, this nifty-looking Mt. Washington saloon is "very sports bar-ish"; the back room, staffed by a "personable" crew, is given over to silk shirtsleeve and business dining of the "steak and garlic potatoes" kind; despite plenty of applause, there's a feeling it hasn't reached its potential.

McGarvey's ◕ S   17 | 18 | 17 | $18

8 Market Space (Pinkney St.), Annapolis, 410-263-5700

◼ An Annapolis 'must' for preppies and naval cadets, with "heavy tourist traffic" too, this nautical pub has a fine house brew, "one of the better raw bars" and "great black-bean soup"; but the real reasons to go here are to soak up "seaport atmosphere" and to "see someone you know."

Mencken's Cultured   ▽ 14 | 11 | 14 | $14
Pearl Cafe S

1116 Hollins St. (Arlington Ave.), 410-837-1947

◪ "Dress arty" to blend in at this "bohemian burrito bar" near the Hollins Market, and don't arrive hungry 'cause "once you get past the chips and salsa", there's not much good to eat; that's "no big deal" because many of the regulars go strictly for the scene.

M. GETTIER 25 | 20 | 24 | $33

505 S. Broadway (bet. Eastern Ave. & Fleet St.), 410-732-1151

■ According to local bec fins this relatively new, "intimate" dining room may be the "best French in Baltimore" – and it's "still improving"; talented chef-owner Michael Gettier gives a contemporary twist to classical cuisine and it would be hard to find more "obliging" help; however, a Fells Point fringe location and limited seating work against it.

Mick's [S] 16 | 17 | 17 | $17

187 Annapolis Mall (Parole Rd.), Annapolis, 410-224-4225
Towson Commons, 425 York Rd. (bet. Pennsylvania & Chesapeake Aves.), Towson, 410-825-0071

See Washington, DC, Alphabetical Directory.

Middleton Tavern ◐ [S] 18 | 19 | 18 | $23

2 Market Space (Randall St.), Annapolis, 410-263-3323 in Baltimore call 410-269-1256, in DC call 301-261-2838

◪ This colonial-era, Annapolis relic is "still good" for an oyster shooter and "fish fare", especially at a "sidewalk table" or in the pubby bar when the "fireplace is lit"; locals who "love this place" save it for a rainy day, but even they admit it needs "refurbishing" and some grown-up help.

Milano's [S] 14 | 8 | 12 | $13

8811 Waltham Woods Rd. (Joppa Rd.), 410-661-4352 💳
2047 York Rd. (Timonium Rd.), Timonium, 410-252-7878
Greenspring Shopping Ctr., 2821 Smith Ave. (bet. Greenspring Ave. & Sanzo Rd.), 410-653-2100

■ For cheap family fill-ups, it's hard to beat these utilitarian pizza, pasta and sub shops with their familiar Greek and Italian choices; they're also handy for a "quick" lunch, but consider them "carry-out only" if you want quiet or decor.

MILTON INN [S] 26 | 26 | 25 | $42

14833 York Rd. (bet. Hunt Valley Mall & Belfast Rd.), Sparks, 410-771-4366

■ Dining fireside in the "hearth room" of this "romantic", "old stone" country mansion is a "delightful", if "expensive", way to make "special occasions more special"; it combines "old-world" cosseting with "New World cooking" and great wines that have reportedly won it the patronage of the USA's No. 1 wine guru, Robert Parker; P.S. upstairs is "Siberia."

Morgan Millard [S] 18 | 18 | 18 | $21

4800 Roland Ave. (bet. Upland & Elmhurst Rds.), 410-889-0030

◪ "The Morg", as it's fondly called in Roland Park, has a "country" look, a "preppy" appeal and is both a "glorified luncheonette" and a "lovely local restaurant"; it's the local drop-in for "healthy" salads, stir-fries and "stylish cooking" from the "'50s"; still, some find it "kind of boring."

Morning Edition Cafe S   ▽ 20 17 14 $14
153 N. Patterson Park Ave. (Fayette St.), 410-732-5133
■ You'll get the "feel" of "Woodstock" at this "artistically dingy", countrified, Highlandtown cafe; it's great for homey lunches and "music" dinners, and is at its best for brunch; but "take the Sunday paper, you'll have time to read it all and cut out the coupons" before being seated and served.

Mo's Crab & Pasta Factory ◗ S ▽ 20 14 18 $23
502-Albemarle St. (Eastern Ave.), 410-837-1600
Mo's Fisherman's Exchange ◗ S
Satyr Hill Shopping Ctr., 2025 E. Joppa Rd. (Satyr Hill Rd.), 410-665-8800
Mo's Fisherman's Wharf Inner Harbor ◗ S
219 President St. (Stiles St.), 410-837-8600
Mo's Seafood Factory ◗ S
7146 Ritchie Hwy. (Furnace Branch Rd.), Glen Burnie, 410-768-1000
■ Aptly named, these piscatorial paradises have industrial-sized portions of the "freshest fish" and pasta, cooked and sauced dozens of ways; the settings are as simple as the concept: "a lot of good, wholesome food for the money."

Mt. Washington Tavern S   14 16 14 $18
5700 Newbury St. (Sulgrave Ave.), 410-367-6903
☑ Baltimore's "homegrown yuppies" hang out at this woody bar with "over 100 beers"; "real adults" have been known to eat here too, though your success with the sea-fare menu depends on whether the kitchen can "get the order right."

New No Da Ji S   ▽ 15 11 16 $20
2501 N. Charles St. (25th St.), 410-235-4846
■ Walking into this dark-looking Upper Charles Street Asian may feel like "a bad acid trip", but experimenting with its "huge Chinese-Korean-Japanese" menu can be very rewarding – fans walk out "singing I'm a Seoul man."

Nickel City Grill S   ▽ 13 17 16 $17
Harborplace, Pratt St. Pavilion, 410-752-0900
☑ Part of the Inner Harbor tourist scene, this shiny grill with an Old Baltimore "twist" placates kids with burgers and a "revolving (electric) train" while their elders enjoy fair pub fare and terrific outdoor and indoor viewspots.

NORTHWOODS S   24 21 23 $31
609 Melvin Ave. (Ridgely Ave.), Annapolis, 410-268-2609, in Baltimore call 410-269-6775
■ Consistently rated "Annapolis' best", this old-world Continental, in an "off-the-tourist-track", residential setting is basically a "nice place to enjoy dinner" with an "outstanding" $22.95 prix fixe; "cramped seating", advance reserving and slightly dated ambiance are part of the deal.

O'Brien's ◗ 🅂 (fka Fran O'Brien's) — | — | — | M
113 Main St. (Green St.), Annapolis, 410-268-6288, in
Baltimore call 410-269-0099, in DC call 301-261-2100
A "political" marketplace by day, this clubby tavern "really
jumps at night" if you're "Mids"(as in Midshipmen)-aged
or younger; new management hasn't changed the "steak-
and-seafood menu", the "just folks" approach or the
happy hour scene, but somehow it's doing them "better."

Obrycki's 🅂   20 | 15 | 17 | $24
1727 E. Pratt St. (bet. Broadway & Register St.), 410-732-6399
🔲 "You have to love Obrycki's" if you're from Baltimore; if
you're not, paying good money for "surly service" while
bashing black-peppered crabs in a "noisy", dimly lit,
utilitarian room may not seem like your fantasy "feeding
frenzy" – but do try it; N.B. don't embarrass yourself by
ordering "other seafood."

Ocean Pride 🅂   15 | 7 | 14 | $17
1534 York Rd. (bet. Seminary Rd. & Bellona Ave.),
Lutherville, 410-321-7744
🔲 Many people's choice for great crabs, buffalo wings
and local, call-you-"hon" ambiance, this bar and seafood
spot is no one's choice for comfort or decor.

Orchard Market & Cafe 🅂   ▽ 20 | 15 | 19 | $19
8815 Orchard Tree Ln. (Joppa Rd.), Towson, 410-339-7700
⬛ Bridging cultural barriers with "delicious, fresh, original"
"inexpensive" food and Middle Eastern courtesy, this
"lovely, informal" Persian cafe/market in Towson is a big
success; locals find Iranian food "different" but also "safe";
"BYOB is a major advantage."

Orchid, The 🅂   20 | 17 | 19 | $26
419 N. Charles St. (Franklin St.), 410-837-0080
⬛ Having pioneered Asian-French fusion cuisine before it
was trendily labeled, this "private, quiet" Mt. Vernon
townhouse still "impresses": "a pleasant place to dine",
"a good meal", "makes you feel special."

OUTBACK STEAKHOUSE 🅂   20 | 17 | 19 | $20
2207 Forest Dr. (Riva Rd.), Annapolis, 410-266-7229
See Washington, DC, Alphabetical Directory.

Palermo's Grill 🅂   ▽ 19 | 20 | 19 | $18
Padonia Park Plaza, 106 W. Padonia Rd. (York Rd.),
Timonium, 410-252-0600
🔲 This good-looking baseball-theme bar and grill is
Timonium's "good addition" for anything from a drink and
bar snacks to serious seafood, garlicky pastas and grills;
and like its namesake, Steve Palermo, it's not just good-
natured, it sponsors charity events and good works.

163

Paolo's ◐ [S] 20 20 19 $22
Harborplace, 301 Light St. Pavilion, 410-539-7060
Towson Commons (York Rd.), Towson, 410-823-4541
See Washington, DC, Alphabetical Directory.

PaperMoon Diner ◐ [S] ≠ – – – I
227 W. 29th St. (bet. Howard & Remington Sts.), 410-889-4444
A playful spirit pervades this funky Hampden house brightened with Crayola bright colors, decoupage and oddments; the same whimsy is apparent in the '50s menu of breakfast all day, salads, soups, sandwiches and "TV dinners"; early reports indicate that they do serious work.

Pavilion at the Walters, The [S] 22 23 20 $25
600 N. Charles St. (Centre St.), 410-727-2233
■ "Better than owning your own villa" is lunching at the Walters Art Gallery; after all, you get the soaring, skylit space, soothing fountain, "elegant" surroundings, "attentive service" and "interesting" modern American food with no insurance, upkeep or staffing headaches; the only benefit of ownership would be shutting out the weekend crowd.

Peabody's Grill [S] ▽ 15 18 17 $22
The Latham Hotel, 612 Cathedral St. (Monument St.), 410-727-7101
◩ Something of a "Downtown find", this everyday restaurant in one of the city's top hotels has a "creaky leather", polished-wood "upscale pub" ambiance and some "very good American food and service"; lately, its performance is said to have been "erratic."

Peerce's Plantation [S] 21 22 21 $29
12450 Dulaney Valley Rd. (Loch Raven Dr.), Phoenix, 410-252-3100
■ In a "tranquil" setting overlooking Loch Raven reservoir, this popular landmark's slow pace and "Southern-style" cooking are reminders that Baltimore was once a quiet Southern town; go for a "good mint julep" in the garden, or special events like its "beautiful Thanksgiving dinner."

Phillips [S] 14 14 14 $22
Harborplace, Light St. Pavilion, 410-685-6600
See Washington, DC, Alphabetical Directory.

Piccolo's at Fells Point [S] – – – E
Brown's Wharf, 1629 Thames St. (Broadway), Fells Point, 410-522-6600
Transforming a perfect location on a Fells Point wharf into a tribute to Tuscany, this upstart's stylized decor sets the tone for upscale treatments of pasta, veal and seafood standards and private label wines; an interesting approach is arriving by boat: take your yacht, or the water taxi.

Pier 5 Clarion Inn [S] 14 | 15 | 14 | $23
(fka Harrison's)
Pier 5 Clarion Inn, 711 Eastern Ave. (bet. President St. & Market Pl.), 410-783-5553
◪ At its best for "crabs on the deck" or on the fishing boat docked at its pier, this mammoth Inner Harbor restaurant "needs a warmer look" inside and less variable "down-home Eastern shore" seafood and service to hook natives more than "once per year"; P.S. you're paying for harborfront real estate and it doesn't come cheap.

Pier 500 [S] 16 | 19 | 18 | $28
HarborView Marina, 500 Harborview Dr. (Key Hwy.), 410-625-0500
◪ Watching the "fun on the water" from this "outstanding" marina location distracts diners from "elbow-to-elbow" inside seating, "lapses in service" and Contemporary American food that wobbles as chefs come and go; its current menu of bar fare, salads, pastas and updated entrees works fine for the kind of free-form eating that's fashionable nowadays.

Pierpoint [S] 23 | 16 | 20 | $29
1822 Aliceanna St. (bet. Ann & Wolfe Sts.), 410-675-2080
■ Nancy Longo, the chef-owner of this Fells Point bistro, is "in the club of Great American Chefs" but is "not adequately recognized" at home; she draws upon her Italian and Maryland heritage to turn the freshest seafood and produce into "inventive", "upscale/down-home" dishes; since her "too small" place is often "crowded", "noisy" and a tad "uneven" when overbusy, go at "off-hours" to experience its "relaxed" best.

POLO GRILL [S] 24 | 23 | 22 | $37
The Inn at the Colonnade, 4 W. University Pkwy. (bet. Canterbury & Charles Sts.), 410-235-8200
■ "If they know you, they love you" at this "classy", very Baltimore brasserie, particularly if you're a major "pol" or a "flashy regular"; however, even if you're a "bum" in their books, once seated you'll be "attentively" served and well-fed by a "smart kitchen" that updates Old Maryland and grill-room classics; N.B. prices are lower at lunch.

PRIME RIB, THE ◐ [S] 26 | 24 | 25 | $41
Horizon House, 1101 N. Calvert St. (Chase St.), 410-539-1804
■ This snazzy-looking Downtowner feels like a sophisticated "NYC East Side hideaway"; it has wonderful "red meat and Manhattans" and this being Maryland "its seafood is superb" too; it perennially gets top ratings and high praise: "first-class all the way", "great to go back to", but to avoid crowds and noise, go midweek.

Puffin's S　　　　　22 | 17 | 20 | $23
1000 Reisterstown Rd. (Sherwood Ave.), Pikesville,
410-486-8811
■ Don't be fooled by its funky "tech" decor; this Pikesville "neighborhood eatery" and its glossy customers take "cardiac-aware feeding" seriously; if you're willing to forgo "red meat" and "artificial substances" in favor of soups, veggies, grills, breads and spreads, you'll find it "enjoyable", if not cheap.

Ralphie's Diner S　　　　13 | 15 | 15 | $18
9690 Deereco Rd. (Padonia Rd.), Timonium, 410-252-3990
☑ You "can always find something to eat" and spot someone you know at this suburban '90s-style diner, which helps make it "fun for drinks after work" or an informal lunch; though its hearty soups, burgers, meat loaf and oversized desserts have their takers, most score the food only "so-so" and the employees, less so.

Raphael's Cucina Italiana S　▽ 23 | 16 | 23 | $26
411 S. High St. (Eastern Ave.), 410-RAP-HAEL
■ At "one of Little Italy's rising stars", the focus is on the "really terrific", "individually prepared" Italian dishes and on making the meal a "pleasant" experience, despite limited space, noise and crowds; don't miss the vintage photos in the downstairs bar.

RED HOT & BLUE S　　　　21 | 15 | 18 | $17
201 Revell Hwy. (Old Mill Bottom Rd.), Annapolis,
410-626-7427
11308 Reisterstown Rd. (High Falcon Rd.), Owings Mills,
410-356-6959
See Washington, DC, Alphabetical Directory.

Red Star, The S　　　　18 | 16 | 16 | $19
906 S. Wolfe St. (Thames St.), 410-327-2212
☑ "Loud on date night" when you may find "better pick-ups" than pickin's because it's "too crowded" to eat, this Fells Point Contemporary American is "great" for a laid-back lunch; with a "variety" of choices, it's all "good."

Regi's S　　　　　▽ 16 | 13 | 17 | $15
1002 Light St. (Hamburg St.), 410-539-7344
■ A "friendly" Federal Hill "neighborhood joint" with a fireplace and warm-hearted owner; it's like a second home to its "clique" who drop by to see what "homey", spicy concoctions are on the Eclectic-American menu that night; word is it also has "some of the best sandwiches (and salads) in town."

RUDYS' 2900 S 24 | 20 | 23 | $33
2900 Baltimore Blvd. (Rte. 91), Finksburg, 410-833-5777
■ Meisterchef Rudy Speckamp keeps reinventing his award-winning Continental-American cuisine, most recently with an "outstanding lighter menu" of mix-and-match starters, pastas and contemporary entrees; most diners love the "excellent" food and "service with a bow", but not the room ("too bright", "noisy") or the drive.

Rusty Scupper S 14 | 17 | 15 | $21
402 Key Hwy. (Light St.), 410-727-3678
☑ The "best Inner Harbor spot" to sit outside on a "balmy day" has "disappointing" seafood, steak and service; this "prime location" is crying out for "someone to take over" and offer food worthy of the "breathtaking" sunsets.

RUTH'S CHRIS STEAK HOUSE S 22 | 20 | 21 | $36
34 Market Place, 600 Water St. (Market Pl.), 410-783-0033
See Washington, DC, Alphabetical Directory.

Sabatino's ◐ S 19 | 15 | 19 | $23
901 Fawn St. (S. High St.), 410-727-9414
■ Little Italy's "famous" "Sabs" defines the Italian-American genre with the "largest servings" of "old-fashioned red-sauce food", late hours and a "relaxing" ambiance that's "like eating with an Italian family"; sure, it's rushed, noisy and crowded and the "food's not that good", but "no one ever got fired for taking a client there."

Sam's Waterfront Cafe S ▽ 19 | 22 | 19 | $20
2020 Chesapeake Harbour Dr. E. (Edgewood Rd.), Annapolis, 410-263-3600
☑ Anchored by an "elegant setting" and an "outstanding water view" near Annapolis, this "pleasant" Contemporary American has been battered by constant management changes; as a result, the "quality of the food varies", though seafood is a good bet "when in season."

Sfuzzi S 19 | 18 | 18 | $21
100 E. Pratt St. (Calvert St.), 410-576-8500
■ A "high-energy", "glitzy" Inner Harbor Nuevo Italian with some "surprisingly good" pastas and "great focaccia"; it draws everyone from business lunchers to romantic couples.

Shogun S ▽ 20 | 15 | 18 | $21
316 N. Charles St. (bet. Saratoga & Pleasant Sts.), 410-962-1130
■ "Go north on Charles and turn left into Tokyo"; this "very civilized" Japanese on Downtown's "Restaurant Row" has a "reliable" sushi bar and cooked dishes served in traditional dining areas; most rate it just "a cut below Kawasaki."

Silver Diner S   14 | 17 | 16 | $14
*Towson Town Ctr., 825 Dulaney Valley Rd. (Fairmont Ave.),
410-823-5566*
See Washington, DC, Alphabetical Directory.

Sisson's S   19 | 17 | 19 | $20
36 E. Cross St. (bet. Light & Charles Sts.), 410-539-2093
■ Serious eaters know that besides its "wonderful"
home-brewed beer", this Federal Hill pub "has excellent
(Cajun-Creole) food" in its dining room upstairs; however,
it's also "a great bar" with a "warm", "dark, cluttered"
feel and "staff who take care of all problems."

Southwest Passage S   ▽ 16 | 17 | 15 | $17
629 S. Broadway (bet. Fleet & Aliceanna Sts.), 410-558-0906
◪ To some, the spicy food at this tidy Fells Point New
Mexican tastes like it would "if a gourmet chef did semi-
vegetarian spa cuisine in Taos"; others shrug: "sometimes
good, sometimes bad", "too small"; its latest craze is
replacing beef with bison and boar; BYOB.

Spike & Charlie's Restaurant S   21 | 18 | 19 | $25
1225 Cathedral St. (Preston St.), 410-752-8144
■ Bringing a "touch of California" chic to a dispirited area
near the "city's two major concert halls", this "up-and-
comer's" casual menu of pizzas, pastas and grills is
enjoyable despite an occasional "kink"; go "off-time" to
relax and sample its "good wines", later for jazz in the club.

Stixx Cafe   ▽ 17 | 13 | 14 | $24
*Club Ctr., 1500 Reisterstown Rd. (bet. McHenry Ave. & Old
Court Rd.), Pikesville, 410-484-7787*
◪ "Fresh sushi" for its eat-near-home Pikesville neighbors,
along with "offbeat" salads, sandwiches and grills is this
informal cafe's shtick – service is "iffy", its appearance,
slick; comments range from "great food" to "overpriced",
"served by snobs."

STONE MILL BAKERY S ⌦   24 | 13 | 14 | $12
1609 Sulgrave Ave. (Kelly Ave.), 410-542-2233
STONE MILL BAKERY & ECOLE
*Greenspring Station, 10751 Falls Rd. (Greenspring Valley Rd.),
Lutherville, 410-821-1358*
■ Demand for these homey bakery/cafe's "superior"
sandwiches (made on "perfect yeasty-crunchy" bread),
as well as for their "innovative salads" and "die-for"
desserts already results in "crowded mayhem at lunch";
don't miss the bistro dinners next door at Ecole, Fridays
and Saturdays only.

Strapazza   14 | 10 | 15 | $17
300 Pratt St. (bet. Howard & Eutaw Sts.), 410-547-1160 S
1330 Reisterstown Rd. (Walker Ave.), Pikesville,
410-484-6906 S
12 W. Allegheny Ave. (York Rd.), Towson, 410-296-5577 S
Palace 9, 8775 Centre Park Dr. (Old Annapolis Rd.),
Columbia, 410-997-6144 S
Riva Festival, 2341 Forest Dr. (Riva Rd.), Annapolis,
410-224-6616 S
201 N. Charles St. (Lexington St.), 410-576-1177
☑ These proliferating pizza and 'pastability' places suffice
for "cheap family" fill-ups, or for a "standard Southern
Italian" lunch; as tacky as they look, "they try"; its latest
scores a hit, decorwise, with a Camden Yards location.

Sushi Cafe S   ▽ 18 | 10 | 16 | $18
1640 Thames St. (Broadway), 410-732-3570
☑ A "hole-in-the-wall" next to Fells Point's Admiral Fell Inn,
this "bargain" sushi spot ain't gourmet, but it's a great late-
night stop if you've drunk enough to accept its "hot pepper
roll challenge" – it's free if you can eat it in 30 seconds.

Szechuan Best S   ▽ 19 | 9 | 17 | $17
8625 Liberty Rd. (Old Court Rd.), Randallstown, 410-521-0020
☑ "Among the best" Chinese, if you know the ropes; order
"from the Chinese-language menu" to sample the "high-
quality" dishes that draw "so many Chinese to this
Americanized"-looking place; the food is "so good" and
prices "so cheap" you "don't notice the fake plants."

TABRIZI'S S   23 | 19 | 21 | $26
1026 S. Charles St. (bet. Cross & Hamburg Sts.), 410-752-3810
■ No wonder people vie for tables at this affordable South
Baltimore Middle Eastern–Eclectic; it serves "delicious,
interesting food" including veggie dishes, and its "intimate"
atrium-lit dining room and patio are "relaxing places to eat."

Taverna Athena S   20 | 20 | 20 | $20
Harborplace, Pratt St. Pavilion, 410-547-8900
■ To show off Baltimore's waterfront vistas and Inner
Harbor people-watching, this lovely Grecian is a natural
choice; while "middle-of-the-harbor" outdoor seating and
floor-to-ceiling window views "make it special", the food's
"pretty darn good", prices "low" and servers are "sweeties."

Tersiguel's S   23 | 21 | 21 | $33
8293 Main St. (Old Columbia Pike), Ellicott City, 410-465-4004
■ It's always a pleasure to watch a pro like Fernand
Tersiguel "make each guest feel at home"; his cozy place
in Ellicott City reeks of garlic and country French charm,
and hums with diners eating heartily and having "fun";
pick an "uncrowded evening" or else sit downstairs.

T.G.I. Friday's ☽ S   14 | 14 | 15 | $15
Towson Town Ctr., 668 Fairmont Ave., Towson, 410-828-4556
Annapolis Harbour Ctr., 2582 Solomons Island Rd.
(Patuxent Blvd.), Annapolis, 410-224-4870
4921 Campbell Blvd. (Honeygo Blvd.), White Marsh,
410-931-3091
Restaurant Park, 5330 Benson Dr., Columbia, 410-312-2719
See Washington, DC, Alphabetical Directory.

Thai S   ▽ 24 | 14 | 19 | $18
3316-18 Greenmount Ave. (33rd St.), 410-889-7303
■ There's nothing fancy about this Waverly storefront, but
it's "obvious why all the food critics love" it: it serves
"fresh Thai food" with "great flavors" at "great prices",
and you can ask the kitchen to "hold the pepper and
chili", or you can have "steam coming out of your ears."

Thai Landing   ▽ 21 | 15 | 19 | $17
1207 N. Charles St. (bet. Biddle & Preston Sts.), 410-727-1234
■ Mt. Vernon Thai that's "more refined and personable"
than most, but doesn't hold back on the heat "if you
convince the waiter you can take it"; attractive decor,
"good service" and realistic prices "give it an edge."

TIO PEPE S   25 | 20 | 21 | $33
10 E. Franklin St. (bet. Charles & St. Paul Sts.), 410-539-4675
◪ This beloved Downtown "classic", with its "cave"-like
decor and "chauvinistic service", feels like a "'50s fancy
restaurant", which "adds odd charm to its good, if old-
fashioned, Spanish" food; far from a has-been, it's extremely
popular: if you go early (as you must, even with so-called
reservations), you'll "have to fight your way out" the door.

Tomato Palace, The S   ▽ 21 | 19 | 20 | $19
10221 Wincopin Circle (Rte. 175), Columbia, 410-715-0211
See Washington, DC, Alphabetical Directory.

Tony Cheng's Szechuan S   20 | 18 | 18 | $22
801 N. Charles St. (Madison St.), 410-539-6666
◪ There are "better and cheaper Chinese elsewhere",
but few offer a "lovely" Mt. Vernon townhouse to relax in;
but its "expensive versions of the usuals" lack "zip", waiters
"intrude" and the place "could use some fresh paint."

Trattoria Alberto   ▽ 23 | 16 | 20 | $34
1660 Crain Hwy. (bet. Hospital Dr. & Underpass Rte. 100),
Glen Burnie, 410-761-0922
◪ "Better and pleasanter" than its grungy Glen Burnie
"strip-center" locale "would suggest", this Northern
Italian offers a pretty pastel interior and "excellent"
cooking; unfortunately, it's sometimes hard to distinguish
helpfulness from "hustle" at these premium prices.

Treaty of Paris 🅂　　　　22 | 23 | 22 | $32
The Maryland Inn, 16 Church Circle (bet. Main & Duke of Gloucester Sts.), Annapolis, 410-263-2641, in Baltimore call 410-269-0990
■ "Classy, in a disorganized way", this "wonderful" 200-year-old Annapolis tavern cleverly blends Old Maryland seafood, veggie fare and contemporary classics in a cozy, "down-at-the-heels" ambiance that charms clients, parents and SOs; its Publik Table feasts offer a real taste of history, and weekend jazz includes the likes of Charlie Byrd.

Uncle Lee's Szechuan 🅂　　　17 | 14 | 16 | $17
44 South St. (E. Lombard St.), 410-727-6666
3313 Greenmount Ave. (33rd St.), 410-366-3333
☑ When it's "on", this Szechuan in a converted Downtown bank cooks like the "premiere Chinese" it "used to be"; but we hear that its quality is "declining" and though still a "good value", takeout is preferred; ditto the Greenmount location.

Vanguard Cafe ◗🅂　　　▽ 19 | 24 | 19 | $20
405 N. Charles St. (Mulberry St.), 410-837-6621
☑ A Downtown living room for the young and the "hip" with a "constantly changing" New American–Eclectic menu, "a chess table, fireplace, sofas" and a roomful of delightfully mismatched period chairs and tiny tables just big enough for sipping "cappuccino while on a date"; "open late", it adds live jazz Wednesday and Thursday.

Waterside 🅂　　　　　▽ 21 | 21 | 20 | $30
The Columbia Inn, 10207 Wincopin Circle (Rte. 175), Columbia, 410-730-3900
■ "Very quiet", "very fancy" and very useful for business entertaining, and for its "excellent Sunday brunch"; on "sunny days" few places are nicer than this "lovely" room with wide-angle water views, soothing decor and well-prepared American food; it gives hotel dining a good name.

Water St. Exchange　　　▽ 18 | 16 | 17 | $18
110 Water St. (bet. Calvert & Light Sts.), 410-332-4060
☑ Victorian-accented Downtown watering hole that's popular for "after-work" boozing and schmoozing and "casual" lunches and dinners of the two-briefcase kind; some say the "atmosphere beats the kitchen", but the "wonderful Caesar salad" is a notable exception.

Weber's on Boston ◗🅂　　18 | 18 | 18 | $22
845 S. Montford Ave. (Boston St.), 410-276-0800
☑ "Young fast foodies moving up" have adopted this classy Canton restoration with its "trendy" bar scene downstairs and "casual elegance" in the dining room above; a new (post-*Survey*) owner promises modern Regional cuisine which should please those who found its old menu "boring."

Westminster Inn S
▽ 21 | 21 | 18 | $28 |

Westminster Inn, 5 S. Center St. (Green St.), Westminster, 410-857-4445, in Baltimore call 410-876-2893

☑ It's a "nice ride" to this Carroll County "suburban inn" where you can cap off the day with a "gourmet" American meal in a greenhouse dining room, drinks in the turn-of-the-century bar, or pub fare in a charming courtyard; its formal, ego-stroking dinner "can be very good", but without a "twofer", it's too costly for some folks.

Windows S
18 | 22 | 20 | $22 |

Stouffer's Harborplace Hotel, 202 E. Pratt St. (South St.), 410-685-VIEW

☑ A "great view of the city" dominates this "excellent all-day" hotel restaurant with everything from a Starbucks coffee bar and an "economical lunch buffet" to the "perfect Maryland crab cake" and Contemporary Regional cuisine; recent reports suggest that it's making a real effort to be more than simply a suitable backdrop for entertaining.

Winterling's S
– | – | – | M |

3200 Foster Ave. (East Ave.), 410-732-7731

This born-again Highlandtown classic is trying to sell Generation X on the simple Maryland-style American fare that its grandparents and great-grandparents fancied; while the bar will take you back to the good old days, the dining rooms have yet to get there.

Woman's Industrial Exchange ⌿
16 | 13 | 19 | $12 |

333 N. Charles St. (Pleasant St.), 410-685-4388

■ "Like Jell-O", the "classic white-bread lunch", chicken salad and "lemonade stirred to order" by "kindly" grandmothers in this Downtown landmark tearoom evoke "heartwarming" memories; at breakfast, a distinguished company steps back "to a more civilized era" over homey muffins as a great "start" to the day; closed at night.

INDEXES TO BALTIMORE RESTAURANTS

SPECIAL FEATURES AND APPEALS

TYPES OF CUISINE

Palermo's Grill
Phillips
Piccolo's
Pier 5
Pier 500
Pierpoint
Polo Grill
Prime Rib
Rusty Scupper
Treaty of Paris
Windows

Southwestern
Lista's
Loco Hombre
Mencken's
Southwest Passage

Spanish
Tio Pepe

Steakhouses
Chart House
Corinthian
CrossRoads
Freds
Hersh's Orchard
McCafferty's
O'Brien's/A
Outback Stkhse.

Polo Grill
Prime Rib
Rusty Scupper
Ruth's Chris

Sushi
Bamboo House
Hoang's
Kawasaki
Matsuri
New No Da Ji
Shogun
Stixx Cafe
Sushi Cafe

Thai
Bangkok Place
Thai
Thai Landing

Vegetarian
Louie's Bookstore
Puffin's
Tabrizi's
Treaty of Paris

Vietnamese
CoChin
Hoang's

NEIGHBORHOOD LOCATIONS

BALTIMORE

Charles Street/ Mount Vernon
Akbar
Al Pacino Cafe
Bombay Grill
Brass Elephant
Citronelle
CoChin
Donna's
Eager House
Gr. Amer. Melt. Pot
Helmand
Henry & Jeff's
Kawasaki
Louie's Bookstore
Orchid, The
Pavilion at Walters
Peabody's Grill
Shogun
Spike & Charlie's
Strapazza
Thai Landing
Tio Pepe
Tony Cheng's
Vanguard Cafe
Woman's Indust. Exch.

Downtown/ Convention Center
Attman's Deli
Boathouse
Bohager's
Burke's Cafe
Marconi's
Martick's
Prime Rib
Ruth's Chris
Strapazza
Uncle Lee's
Water St. Exchange

Inner Harbor
American Cafe
Baltimore Brewing Co.
Bamboo House
Berry & Elliot's
Chart House
Hampton's
Nickel City Grill
Paolo's

Phillips
Pier 5
Pier 500
Rusty Scupper
Sfuzzi
Taverna Athena
Windows

Little Italy
Amicci's
Boccaccio
Caesar's Den
Chiapparelli's
Dalesio's
Da Mimmo
Germano's
Mo's
Raphael's
Sabatino's

Fells Point/East Baltimore
Al Pacino Cafe
Bay Cafe
Bertha's
BOP
Foster's
Haussner's
Henninger's
Ikaros
John Steven Ltd.
Lista's
M. Gettier
Morning Edition
Obrycki's
Piccolo's
Pierpoint
Red Star
Southwest Passage
Sushi Cafe
Weber's
Winterling's

Federal Hill/ South-Southwest Baltimore
Banjara
Cafe Manet
Gunning's
Gypsy's Cafe

Matsuri
Mencken's
Regi's
Sisson's
Tabrizi's

Roland Park/Waverly/ Remington

Alonso's
Ambassador Room
Benny's
Cafe Hon
Donna's at BMA
Jeannier's
Ledo Pizza
Loco Hombre
Morgan Millard
New No Da Ji
PaperMoon
Polo Grill
Thai
Uncle Lee's

Mt. Washington/ Lutherville/Cross Keys

CrossRoads
Harvey's
Hoang's
McCafferty's
Mt. Washington Tavern
Stone Mill Bakery
Stone Mill Bkry./Ecole

Towson/Northeast Baltimore County

Al Pacino Cafe
American Cafe
Angelina's
Bangkok Place
Bertucci's
Bo Brooks
Cafe Troia
Donna's
Fisherman's Wharf
Hersh's Orchard
Mick's
Milano's
Mo's
Orchard Market
Paolo's
Silver Diner
Strapazza
T.G.I. Friday's

Timonium/Cockeysville/ Hunt Valley

Bamboo House
Gibby's
Ledo Pizza
Milano's
Ocean Pride
Palermo's Grill
Ralphie's Diner

Northern Baltimore County

Manor Tavern
Milton Inn
Peerce's Plantation

Owings Mills/Pikesville/ Randallstown

Akbar
American Cafe
Bertucci's
Due
Fiori
Jasper's
Linwood's
Milano's
Puffin's
Red Hot & Blue
Stixx Cafe
Strapazza
Szechuan Best

Reisterstown/Westminster/ Carroll County

Baugher's
Friendly Farms
Harryman House
Jasper's
Ledo Pizza
Rudys' 2900
Westminster Inn

Ellicott City

Bare Bones
Cacao Lane
Crab Shanty
Il Giardino
Tersiguel's

Columbia

American Cafe
Bertucci's
Bombay Peacock
Clyde's
Cover to Cover Cafe
Kings Contrivance

SPECIAL FEATURES AND APPEALS

Breakfast

(All major hotels
and the following)
Attman's Deli
Baugher's
Burke's Cafe
Cafe Hon
Cafe Normandie
Corinthian
Donna's
Henry & Jeff's
Louie's Bookstore
Morning Edition
PaperMoon
Silver Diner
Stone Mill Bakery
Woman's Indust. Exch.

Brunch

(*Some good bets)
Akbar
Ambassador Room*
Bertha's
Bay Cafe
Benny's
Cafe Hon
Carrols Creek*
Chart House (Annapolis)*
Citronelle*
Corinthian
Cover to Cover Cafe
CrossRoads
Donna's
Foster's
Gr. Amer. Melt. Pot
Gypsy's Cafe
Hampton's*
Harry Browne's
Harryman House*
Harvey's
Henry & Jeff's
Hersh's Orchard
Jasper's
John Steven Ltd.*
Josef's
Lista's*
Loco Hombre
Louie's Bookstore
Manor Tavern*
Marmaduke's/A
Mencken's
Mick's

Middleton Tavern
Morning Edition
Morgan Millard
Mt. Washington Tavern*
O'Brien's/A
Orchard Market
Paolo's*
Pavilion at Walters*
Peabody's Grill
Peerce's Plantation*
Pier 500
Pier 5
Pierpoint*
Polo Grill*
Ralphie's Diner
Red Star
Regi's
Rusty Scupper
Sam's Waterfront*
Sisson's*
Spike & Charlie's*
Szechuan Best
T.G.I. Friday's
Treaty of Paris*
Vanguard Cafe
Waterside
Weber's*

Buffet Served

(Check prices,
days and times)
Akbar
American Cafe
Banjara
Bombay Grill
CoChin
New No Da Ji
Phillips
Windows

Business Dining

Bamboo House
Berry & Elliot's
Brass Elephant
Chiapparelli's
Citronelle
Corinthian
CrossRoads
Due
Fiori
Hersh's Orchard
Kawasaki
Kings Contrivance

Marmaduke's/A (cabaret)
McCafferty's (piano/big band)
Middleton Tavern (piano)
Morning Edition (folk/classical)
Nickel City Grill (jazz)
O'Brien's/A (jazz/dance bands)
Phillips (piano)
Piccolo's (piano)
Pier 5 (bands)
Pier 500 (bands)
Prime Rib (piano)
Rusty Scupper (D.J.)
Treaty of Paris (jazz)
Vanguard Cafe (jazz)
Windows (piano/trios)

Delivers*/Takeout

(Nearly all Asians,
coffee shops, delis,
diners and pizzerias
deliver or do takeout;
here are some best bets;
D = delivery, T = takeout)
Ambassador Room (D,T)
American Cafe (T)
Amicci's (T)
Angelina's (T)
Bare Bones (T)
Baugher's (T)
Benny's (T)
Boathouse (T)
Bo Brooks (T)
Bohager's (T)
Brass Elephant (T)
Burke's Cafe (T)
Cacao Lane (T)
Cafe Hon (T)
Cafe Manet (D,T)
Cafe Normandie (T)
Cafe Troia (T)
Cantler's Riverside (T)
Chiapparelli's (T)
Corinthian (D,T)
Cover to Cover Cafe (T)
Crab Shanty (T)
Dalesio's (T)
Donna's (T)
Eager House (T)
Fisherman's Wharf (T)
Foster's (T)
Freds (T)
Friendly Farms (T)
Germano's (T)
Gibby's (T)
Gunning's (T)

Gypsy's Cafe (T)
Harvey's (D,T)
Haussner's (T)
Helmand (T)
Henninger's (T)
Hersh's Orchard (T)
Il Giardino (T)
Jeannier's (T)
John Steven Ltd. (T)
Josef's (T)
Kings Contrivance (T)
Linwood's (D,T)
Lista's (T)
Little Campus Inn (T)
Loco Hombre (T)
Louie's Bookstore (T)
Mama Lucia (T)
Manor Tavern (T)
Marmaduke's/A (T)
Mencken's (D,T)
Morgan Millard (T)
Morning Edition (T)
Mo's (T)
Nickel City Grill (T)
Northwoods/A (D)
Obrycki's (T)
Ocean Pride (T)
Orchid, The (T)
Outback Stkhse. (T)
Palermo's Grill (T)
Peerce's Plantation (D,T)
Phillips (T)
Piccolo's (T)
Pier 5 (T)
Pier 500 (T)
Pierpoint (T)
Polo Grill (T)
Puffin's (D,T)
Raphael's (T)
Red Hot & Blue (T)
Regi's (T)
Rudys' 2900 (T)
Rusty Scupper (T)
Sisson's (T)
Southwest Passage (T)
Spike & Charlie's (T)
Stone Mill Bakery (T)
Tio Pepe (T)
Treaty of Paris (T)
Vanguard Cafe (T)
Westminster Inn (T)
Woman's Indust. Exch. (T)
(* Call to check range and
charges, if any)

Dessert & Ice Cream

Baugher's
Cafe Hon
Citronelle
Donna's
Due
Friendly Farms
Haussner's
Henninger's
Linwood's
Louie's Bookstore Cafe
Marconi's
PaperMoon
Pierpoint
Polo Grill
Ralphie's Diner
Stone Mill Bakery

Dining Alone

(In addition to hotels
and places with
counter service)
Cafe Hon
Cafe Manet
Cafe Troia
Cover to Cover Cafe
Donna's
Gypsy's Cafe
Lista's
Louie's Bookstore
Pavilion at Walters
Sushi Cafe
Vanguard Cafe

Fireplaces

(* Check locations)
Bay Cafe
Bertha's
Bombay Grill
Bombay Peacock
Cacao Lane
Cafe Normandie
Chart House*
Crab Shanty
Da Mimmo
Eager House
Fiori
Foster's
Gypsy's Cafe
Inn at Perry Cabin
Jasper's*
La Piccola Roma
Manor Tavern
Middleton Tavern
Milton Inn

Mt. Washington Tavern
O'Brien's/A
Ocean Pride
Peerce's Plantation
Tony Cheng's
Treaty of Paris
Uncle Lee's*

Health/Spa Menus

(Most places cook
to order to meet
any dietary request;
call in advance to
check; almost all
Health Food spots,
Chinese, Indian and
other ethnics have
health-conscious meals,
as do the following)
Bo Brooks
Corinthian
Dalesio's
Fiori
Fisherman's Wharf
Germano's
Gr. Amer. Melt. Pot
Harvey's
Henry & Jeff's
Hersh's Orchard
Jasper's
Loco Hombre
Marmaduke's/A
Matsuri
Morning Edition
Mt. Washington Tavern
Paolo's
Pier 500
Piccolo's
Pierpoint
Regi's
Rudys' 2900
Sfuzzi
T.G.I. Friday's
Westminster Inn

Historic Interest

(Year Opened)
1740 Milton Inn*
1750 Middleton Tavern
1767 Fiori*
1770 Treaty of Paris*
1790 Harryman House*
1815 Inn at Perry Cabin*
1820 Bertha's*
1820 La Piccola Roma*

1850 Pavilion at Walters*
1857 Donna's (Downtown)*
1860 Cacao Lane*
1860 Weber's*
1880 Manor Tavern*
1880 Marconi's*
1890 Little Campus Inn*
1890 Tersiguel's*
1896 Morgan Millard*
1899 Westminster Inn*
1900 Kings Contrivance*
1900 Orchid, The*
1904 Vanguard Cafe*
1910 Woman's Indust. Exch.
1926 Haussner's
1931 Ambassador Room
1933 Attman's Deli
1941 Peerce's Plantation
1944 Obrycki's
1948 Baugher's
1955 Sabatino's
(* Building)

Hotel Dining
Columbia Inn
    Waterside, The
Cross Keys Inn
    CrossRoads
Harbor Court Hotel
    Hampton's
Hyatt Regency Baltimore
    Berry & Elliot's
Inn at Perry Cabin
    Inn at Perry Cabin
Inn at the Colonnade
    Polo Grill
Latham Hotel
    Citronelle
    Peabody's
Loews Annapolis
    Corinthian
Maryland Inn
    Treaty of Paris
Pier 5 Clarion Inn
    Pier 5 Clarion Inn
Stouffer's Harborplace Hotel
    Windows
Westminster Inn
    Westminster Inn

"In" Places
Berry & Elliot's
Bertha's
Bohager's
Due
Gr. Amer. Melt. Pot

Gypsy's Cafe
Hersh's Orchard
John Steven Ltd.
Linwood's
Marmaduke's/A
McCafferty's
O'Brien's/A
Orchid, The
Paolo's
Pierpoint
Polo Grill
Prime Rib
Sabatino's
Sisson's
Tio Pepe
Vanguard Cafe
Weber's

Jacket Required
Boccaccio
Hampton's
Marconi's
Prime Rib
Tio Pepe

Late Late – After 12:30
(All hours are AM)
Bay Cafe (1)
Berry & Elliot's (1)
BOP (3)
Burke's Cafe (1:30)
Caesar's Den (1)
Da Mimmo (1)
Donna's (1)
Gr. Amer. Melt. Pot (3)
Gypsy's Cafe (1)
Henry & Jeff's (2)
Jasper's (1)
John Steven Ltd. (1)
Louie's Bookstore (2)
McGarvey's (1:30)
Milano's (2)
Mo's (1:30)
PaperMoon (24 hrs.)
Paolo's (2)
Sabatino's (3)
Silver Diner (3)
Sushi Cafe (2)
T.G.I. Friday's (1)
Vanguard Cafe (1)
Weber's (1)

Noteworthy Newcomers (9)
Benny's
Bertucci's
Boathouse

Donna's at BMA
Loco Hombre
Palermo's Grill
PaperMoon
Piccolo's
Winterling's

Noteworthy Closings (11)

Cafe Normandie
Churchill's
Conrad's
Eureka
Francie's
Grill 58
Harvey House
Tell Tale Hearth
Torremolino's
Truffles
2110

Offbeat

Bertha's
Cafe Hon
Gr. Amer. Melt. Pot
Gypsy's Cafe
Haussner's
John Steven Ltd.
Louie's Bookstore
Martick's
Obrycki's
PaperMoon
Sushi Cafe
Vanguard Cafe
Woman's Indust. Exch.

Outdoor Dining

(G = Garden;
P = Patio;
S = Sidewalk;
T = Terrace;
W = Waterside;
*check locations)
Al Pacino Cafe (S)*
Ambassador Room (G)
American Cafe (P,W)*
Bamboo House (P,W)*
Bay Cafe (P,W)
Benny's (P)
Bertucci's (P)*
Boathouse (P)
Bohager's (P)
Bombay Peacock (P)
Cacao Lane (P)
Cafe Troia (S)
Calif. Pizza Kit. (P)

Cantler's Riverside (P,W)
Carrols Creek (P,W)
Chart House (P,W)*
Cover to Cover Cafe (S)
Donna's (S,T)*
Donna's at BMA (G)
Fiori (P)
Germano's (S)
Gunning's (G)*
Gypsy's Cafe (G)
Harryman House (P)
Harvey's (P)
Henry & Jeff's (S)
Inn at Perry Cabin (T,W)
John Steven Ltd. (T)
Josef's (P)
La Piccola Roma (S)
Ledo Pizza (P)*
Lista's (P,W)
Louie's Bookstore (G)
Mama Lucia (S)
Manor Tavern (T)
Matsuri (S)
Middleton Tavern (S)
Milton Inn (P)
Mo's (P)*
Nickel City Grill (P,W)
Northwoods/A (T)
Palermo's Grill (S)
Paolo's (P)*
PaperMoon (S)
Peabody's Grill (S)
Peerce's Plantation (P)
Phillips (P)
Piccolo's (P,W)
Pier 5 (P,W)
Pier 500 (P,W)
Rusty Scupper (P,W)
Sam's Waterfront (P,W)
Sfuzzi (P)
Southwest Passage (P)
Spike & Charlie's (P)
Stixx Cafe (P)
Strapazza (S)*
Taverna Athena (P,W)
T.G.I. Friday's (P)*
Tomato Palace (P,W)
Vanguard Cafe (S)
Waterside (W)
Water St. Exchange (S)

Outstanding Views

American Cafe
Bamboo House
Bay Cafe

Parties & Private Rooms

(Any nightclub or restaurant
charges less at off hours;
* indicates private rooms
available; best of many)

Baltimore Indexes

Teas

Teenagers & Other Youthful Spirits

Visitors on Expense Accounts

Wheelchair Access

Baltimore Indexes

Finksburg
Rudys' 2900
Loch Raven
Peerce's Plantation
Monkton
Manor Tavern
Reisterstown
Harryman House
Sparks
Milton Inn
St. Michaels
Inn at Perry Cabin
Upperco
Friendly Farms
Westminster
Westminster Inn

Young Children
(Besides the normal
fast-food places)
American Cafe
Attman's Deli
Baltimore Brewing Co.
Bare Bones
Baugher's

Bertucci's
Cantler's Riverside
Chart House
Chiapparelli's
Crab Shanty
Freds
Friendly Farms
Harvey's
Haussner's
Ledo Pizza
Loco Hombre
Mama Lucia
Milano's
Nickel City Grill
Obrycki's
Paolo's
Ralphie's Diner
Red Hot & Blue
Sabatino's
Silver Diner
T.G.I. Friday's
Tomato Palace
Uncle Lee's

Rating Sheets

To aid in your participation in our next *Survey*

F | D | S | C

⌐⌐⌐⌐

Restaurant Name _____
Phone _____
Comments _____
_____
_____

⌐⌐⌐⌐

Restaurant Name _____
Phone _____
Comments _____
_____
_____

⌐⌐⌐⌐

Restaurant Name _____
Phone _____
Comments _____
_____
_____

⌐⌐⌐⌐

Restaurant Name _____
Phone _____
Comments _____
_____
_____

⌐⌐⌐⌐

Restaurant Name _____
Phone _____
Comments _____
_____
_____

⌐⌐⌐⌐

Restaurant Name _____
Phone _____
Comments _____
_____
_____

F | D | S | C |

⌐⌐⌐⌐

Restaurant Name _____
Phone _____
Comments _____
_____
_____

⌐⌐⌐⌐

Restaurant Name _____
Phone _____
Comments _____
_____
_____

⌐⌐⌐⌐

Restaurant Name _____
Phone _____
Comments _____
_____
_____

⌐⌐⌐⌐

Restaurant Name _____
Phone _____
Comments _____
_____
_____

⌐⌐⌐⌐

Restaurant Name _____
Phone _____
Comments _____
_____
_____

⌐⌐⌐⌐

Restaurant Name _____
Phone _____
Comments _____
_____
_____

                                        F D S C
⌐⌐⌐⌐
Restaurant Name _____
Phone _____
Comments _____
_____
_____

⌐⌐⌐⌐
Restaurant Name _____
Phone _____
Comments _____
_____
_____

⌐⌐⌐⌐
Restaurant Name _____
Phone _____
Comments _____
_____
_____

⌐⌐⌐⌐
Restaurant Name _____
Phone _____
Comments _____
_____
_____

⌐⌐⌐⌐
Restaurant Name _____
Phone _____
Comments _____
_____
_____

⌐⌐⌐⌐
Restaurant Name _____
Phone _____
Comments _____
_____
_____

F | D | S | C

⌐⌐⌐⌐

Restaurant Name _____
Phone _____
Comments _____
_____
_____

⌐⌐⌐⌐

Restaurant Name _____
Phone _____
Comments _____
_____
_____

⌐⌐⌐⌐

Restaurant Name _____
Phone _____
Comments _____
_____
_____

⌐⌐⌐⌐

Restaurant Name _____
Phone _____
Comments _____
_____
_____

⌐⌐⌐⌐

Restaurant Name _____
Phone _____
Comments _____
_____
_____

⌐⌐⌐⌐

Restaurant Name _____
Phone _____
Comments _____
_____
_____

F D S C

⌐ ⌐ ⌐ ⌐

Restaurant Name _____
Phone _____
Comments _____
_____
_____

⌐ ⌐ ⌐ ⌐

Restaurant Name _____
Phone _____
Comments _____
_____
_____

⌐ ⌐ ⌐ ⌐

Restaurant Name _____
Phone _____
Comments _____
_____
_____

⌐ ⌐ ⌐ ⌐

Restaurant Name _____
Phone _____
Comments _____
_____
_____

⌐ ⌐ ⌐ ⌐

Restaurant Name _____
Phone _____
Comments _____
_____
_____

⌐ ⌐ ⌐ ⌐

Restaurant Name _____
Phone _____
Comments _____
_____
_____

F | D | S | C

⎿⎿⎿⎿

Restaurant Name _____
Phone _____
Comments _____
_____
_____

⎿⎿⎿⎿

Restaurant Name _____
Phone _____
Comments _____
_____
_____

⎿⎿⎿⎿

Restaurant Name _____
Phone _____
Comments _____
_____
_____

⎿⎿⎿⎿

Restaurant Name _____
Phone _____
Comments _____
_____
_____

⎿⎿⎿⎿

Restaurant Name _____
Phone _____
Comments _____
_____
_____

⎿⎿⎿⎿

Restaurant Name _____
Phone _____
Comments _____
_____
_____

Wine Vintage Chart 1982-1993

These ratings are designed to help you select wine to go with your meal. They are on the same 0–to–30 scale used throughout this *Survey*. The ratings reflect both the quality of the vintage and the wine's readiness to drink. Thus if a wine is not fully mature or is over the hill, its rating has been reduced. The ratings were prepared principally by our friend Howard Stravitz, a law professor at the University of South Carolina.

WHITES	'82	'83	'85	'86	'87	'88	'89	'90	'91	'92	'93
French:											
Burgundy	23	15	28	29	13	23	29	25	17	26	20
Loire Valley	—	—	18	17	13	18	25	24	17	15	18
Champagne	27	23	28	24	—	—	26	25	—	—	—
Sauternes	—	28	21	26	—	27	26	23	—	—	—
California:											
Chardonnay	—	—	—	—	—	26	19	27	25	28	27
REDS											
French:											
Bordeaux	29	26	28	26	16	25	27	25	18	20	23
Burgundy	19	20	28	12	21	25	26	28	21	24	22
Rhône	15	25	26	21	14	27	27	25	18	16	19
Beaujolais	—	—	—	—	—	20	25	22	24	18	23
California:											
Cabernet/ Merlot	23	14	27	25	25	15	20	25	24	23	23
Zinfandel	—	—	18	17	20	15	16	19	19	18	18
Italian:											
Chianti	16	13	27	15	—	24	—	25	—	—	—
Piedmont	25	—	26	11	18	21	26	26	—	—	19

Bargain sippers take note: Some wines are reliable year in, year out, and are reasonably priced as well. These wines are best bought in the most recent vintages. They include: Alsatian Pinot Blancs, Côtes du Rhône, Muscadet, Bardolino, Valpolicella and inexpensive Spanish Rioja and California Zinfandel. (Also: we do not include 1984 because, except for California red wines, the vintage is not recommended.)